Social Media Marketing 2020

A Guide to Brand Building Using Instagram, YouTube, Facebook, Twitter, and Snapchat, Including Specific Advice on Personal Branding for Beginners

Contents

Part 1: Social Media Marketing

An Essential Guide to Building a Brand Using Facebook, YouTube, Instagram, Snapchat, and Twitter, Including Tips on Personal Branding, Advertising and Using Influencers

Introduction

You know why you are here. You're aware of the importance of social media marketing and its potential in 2020, and want to use this amazing tool to strategize content for brand recognition and more sales. But how exactly do you do that, and where do you start?

In this book, you will find up-to-date tips and tricks, along with expert strategies that will help your brand make its mark across social media platforms this year. Even though it contains a few advanced approaches, it is a straightforward read that'll help you maneuver through the hardest gimmicks effortlessly.

Any business today turns to social media to accelerate their performance and engage more customers, which is wise. But there is so much going on with social media platforms right now—like the introduction of new features every year, brands using maximum creativity to engage their followers, and the rise of new companies and influencers carving their niche—that it can feel overwhelming to try and stand out in such a saturated market. This is where this book will come to your rescue. Every page consists of well-versed tactics that will change the way you interact with your customers, helping you create a brand image that you would otherwise not have imagined.

If you are just starting out—or simply thinking of starting out—with social media marketing, you might not know the importance of these platforms. You might also have asked yourself, "Is social media really important for my business?" The answer to this question is always, "Yes!" Social media marketing is necessary for every discipline thriving today. On the other hand, if you're a prominent marketer or an entrepreneur who is familiar with the world of social media, you already know that the majority of your customers use it, and it offers you the opportunity of generating more sales. So, why not use these free tools to your advantage?

Social media can provide you and your brand with several benefits, some of which include building a brand image, spreading your brand's products and principles across the world, unlocking your creative potential, offering better customer service, showing your brand's authenticity, and building your presence in today's digital world. Your website and social media accounts are the first things that your customers are going to check before trusting your products and services, and you have landed on the right book to help you create that great first online impression.

It is time to take social media more seriously and think of it as more than just a fad. No wonder there are specialized courses on it, and job openings that request social media managers and strategists to take over a company's social media department. This book will help you gain insight into many professional tips that will allow you to handle your brand's social media marketing by yourself without having to hire expert teams. By using this blank canvas, you can create your own community or cult and follow your own style while doing so. It guides you through the challenges of presenting the best content you have to offer.

Read on to excel in social media marketing and brand building in 2020, with this thorough blueprint for success.

Chapter 1: Why Is Social Media (Still) Important?

On any given day, at any given time, you will always find people staring at their phones, scrolling through social media. Social media has become a virtual world for each person to escape into, and they get to customize it according to the people and pages they choose to follow. So, if you are asking why social media is important, here are a few facts to set the record straight.

Why social media? Well, because the use of social media around the world is constantly on the rise. Since 2004, the number of users has increased every year, making it an easy resource that needs to be taken advantage of. You would be surprised to know that, in 2019, the number of Internet users spiked by a whopping 9.1 percent to a total of 4.388 billion users. Can you imagine having all these people at reach and not trying to make the most of it for your business? Not only that but of those Internet users, 3.484 billion were on social media 9 percent more than they were the year before. One of the main reasons why social media is so accessible is because smartphones have made it possible for people to access any application with just a click of a button.

So, the next question to ask here is: *How can social media be beneficial for a business?* Well, read on to learn about the advantages of using social media for professional purposes.

Connecting to Potential Customers

One of the best ways to familiarize customers with your company and what it has to offer is through social media. With many people using social media daily, it is easier to target your customers and reach them where they are most likely to be; on their social media platforms. An average person spends at least two hours and 22 minutes per day on social networks, scrolling through their feed, messaging their friends, and trying to post the perfect breakfast photo.

Because of the amount of time spent on social media, it has become a vital resource to capitalize on in order to reach the right audience. Depending on your target audience and what product or service your company offers, the importance of each platform will differ in finding potential customers. However, to maintain a strong image, you must have a strong online presence, which leads to the next point.

Improving Your Reputation

Imagine scrolling through your feed, and a sponsored post of something you are actually interested in comes up. What is the first thing you do? Click on the post and take a glance at the account, of course. In that split second, the number of followers your business account has will have a strong impact on whether or not the user will continue to scroll through your feed.

Unfortunately, social media has given users the ability to judge a book by its cover—in this case, the number of followers and posts, the amount of interaction, and the overall appearance of your social media account. These will instantly be an indication of how legitimate your business is and whether it is worth taking the time to check out the feed or not. It's sad that it's come to this, but it is what it is, and as a business owner, you need to ensure that your online presence is a good indication of your reputable business. You should make sure that your online presence is strong enough to make potential customers stay.

Social Media Marketing

Is social media marketing still a thing? Yes, it is! And it's still as effective as ever. However, before investing in social media marketing, you need to familiarize yourself with two things: understanding the algorithm of the platform you are using to advertise and optimizing the tools to your advantage by targeting the audience correctly to reach the demographics, age, gender, and other specifications you can use to filter your audience.

With social media marketing, you will be able to reach a wider range of users with better stakes, as it is more targeted and directed at actual users who seem to fit the right profile. Not only that, but it's also a cheaper medium as you manage to allocate a very small budget per post instead of spending hefty sums on other forms of marketing and advertisement. In the following chapters, you will be provided with a detailed explanation of how to use each social media platform to your advantage, and which platform will be more suitable for your business type.

Improving Your SEO

Optimizing your SEO is important to give your business the possibility of being seen on the first couple of pages of a Google search. Using the right keywords on your website is just one way to optimize your SEO ranking on Google and make your website or social media platforms more visible. However, another way to gain advantage and direct more traffic to your website is by using social media. Because SEO ranking also factors in usability and the engagement that takes place on your company's social platforms, it recognizes engagement as an indication of your business's reliability, giving it a further push in terms of SEO.

The more present you are on social media, the more likely it is to grab a potential customer's attention and have that potential customer head to your company's website or profile to find out more. This not only gets you more clicks on your website—increasing the SEO ranking—but also paves the way for your customers to reach your products or services and takes them one step closer to making a purchase. That is why it is essential to make your content relatable, engaging, and appealing to your target audience, while always optimizing the necessary keywords to boost your SEO and make your business easier for new customers to find.

Customer Reviews

While some people view a business' social media accounts to get an idea of what they have to offer, others use them to get feedback in terms of the business's products or services. Social media has made it easier for people to voice their opinions without feeling embarrassed, as it is not done in person but through a virtual platform where you never have to meet the people that you are criticizing or praising.

Say a potential customer comes across your products and is interested in buying them; instead of making deciding on a whim, it is quite likely that they will visit your social media platforms and see if any customers have left reviews, or even scroll through your posts to check if there are any negative or positive comments from previous users. The feedback they encounter will gravely affect their decision; it will either help remove the doubts and skepticism they have and encourage them to make a purchase, or put them off entirely and make you lose a customer for good. That is why it is imperative that you handle customer feedback with care and always ensure that your business responds to any negative feedback with professionalism. You need to handle the situation as wisely as possible to prevent it from having an impact on other customers and ruining the reputation of your business. Remember that customer feedback is a double-edged sword that has the power to make or break your reputation and affect your business accordingly.

Building Relationships with Your Customers

Being active on social media allows your customers to get a better understanding of your identity, not only through the products or services you offer but also the tone of voice you use. This helps them relate to your business more and therefore becomes more interactive. When a customer sees your posts frequently and interacts with them regularly, a virtual relationship is formed, making their connection to your brand stronger. Using this concept to your advantage will help you generate better content on social media and allow you to get to know your clients on a personal level.

Social media gives you the ability to monitor and analyze what resonates with the customers and helps you improve your products, services, and social media posts to suit their tastes. The more appealing the content, the stronger the relationship with your customers. In turn, you will be able to have insight into their interests, characters, and what they are drawn to. You'll also realize that as the bond gets stronger, the customer's sense of loyalty toward your brand will increase, making them more inclined to stick with your products instead of those of your competitors.

Social Media is Playful and Fun

There is so much to do on social media besides posting pictures and videos. You can launch interactive social media campaigns—giving your audience a chance to engage in creating videos, take quizzes, or shoot creative photographs of themselves using your products. This not only gives your audience the chance to get creative and enjoy themselves through your brand but also helps them promote your business through their own social media channels as they tag their friends or post whatever they have created on their platforms.

With social media, you have the freedom to try out different mediums, making your brand get identified as fun, interactive, and enjoyable to follow. It also allows you to be timely and use trending topics to your advantage in a playful way that makes your brand even more appealing to your audience. Besides, allowing people to engage with your content in order to get a reward is a great, cheap marketing option that is extremely easy and effective, thanks to social media.

Boosting Sales

If you want to boost your sales, it is not enough to just have a website. Using social media can really help generate more sales as it tends to humanize your brand and increase brand loyalty, as well as reach a wider audience. Instead of having customers come to you, social media allows you to penetrate their feeds. As users scroll through their feeds and see your business's posts, they are constantly reminded of the products or services you offer, keeping your brand on their minds. This allows them to accumulate more knowledge about your brand and products, and easily recommend it to those around them when asked about a company that provides your services. The more exposure your business gets on social media, the higher the number of sales you will generate.

Collaborating with Other Organizations

Because everyone is connected on social media, it makes it fairly easy for your business to reach out to potential companies you feel are a good match and join forces in a collaboration to bring something innovative, exciting, and new to your customers. Not only that, but you can also gain access to a completely different target audience—or reach a wider one—by collaborating with social media influencers and having them promote your brand or engage in a specific campaign.

There are so many ways that social media can be beneficial for business purposes. This makes it not only useful but imperative for a company to have a strong social media presence and really put effort into capitalizing on social media marketing. It is an easy, effective tool that requires minimal resources and generates excellent results, as well as detailed information and analysis to help ensure that your business is moving in the right direction according to what the market needs.

Chapter 2: Changes to Expect in 2020

While the past decade has witnessed a phenomenal rise in social media usage and heavy traffic, content marketers and agencies are rapidly gaining benefits from it. Social media was merely used for entertainment and sharing users' favorite moments in the beginning, but it has now become a major business tool for companies in almost all disciplines. A chunk of the world population has made social media their full-time job, making millions out of creating and sharing content.

Aside from various employment opportunities, social media platforms are also giving people a chance to showcase their talent to the world. Companies are now making sales through social media like never before. And this is only going to increase this year and beyond—so much so that companies are hiring social media managers and content marketers just to handle their social media platforms. While the millennials are already hitting the bullseye, Gen Z is ready to take over the commercial discipline, adding to the inventiveness and originality of social media marketing facets across various platforms.

In 2020, social media will continue to flourish, although many changes are expected. You, too, can benefit from these. This chapter will focus on all the changes that might occur this year, some of which can be directed entirely toward increasing engagement. The year 2017 witnessed a massive growth in social media users, with around one million people joining various platforms every day, and it does not seem to be stopping anytime soon. With this increasing engagement, social media platforms, such as Facebook, Instagram, YouTube, Snapchat, and Twitter, are rapidly experimenting with specific technical changes that can improve user experience. These changes are also being implemented due to privacy breaches, an increase in fake accounts, hackers, and the transmission of fake news.

You need to be aware of these algorithm changes, as they can significantly affect your marketing process.

Changes to Expect Across All Social Media Platforms

Social media can collectively experience some changes this year, with some of the platforms making a few standard modifications. This will not only affect the habits of users but also massively change marketing strategies and business approaches.

Everyone saw Instagram and Facebook adding the feature of stories a few years ago, taking over Snapchat's entire engagement concept, which has now become a big-time engagement tactic for increasing followers and likes. This is because stories were developed for easy access, uplifting the user's experience. Stories are temporarily produced, visually interactive content, and it is easy for users to view the enlarged content without having to rotate the phone. These aspects are mainly what made stories a major hit as a feature. And so, many bloggers use them as a creative way of storytelling, keeping their followers engaged.

This is a good example of how social media platforms are realizing the importance of user mindset and suggesting a few feature changes by implementing several technological advancements and artificial intelligence.

Increased Privacy

The use of social media has exposed people's personal lives to the public, which can be threatening. With the recent Facebook data breach accusations, the social media platform is on its way toward developing a more secure and private network, which can be expected by the end of this year. Not only Facebook, but many leading platforms are alarmed and cautious about increasing privacy to generate better numbers and ratings. When you sign up for any social media platform, you need to fill in general information that is being stored by the respective companies. While this cannot be entirely avoided, people are keen to know the steps these giants are taking to promise better security. This will not only establish brand trust but also induce a feeling of enhanced regulations for the people who are currently on major channels.

Focus on Improved Algorithms

For any social media platform to be successful, the artificial intelligence algorithm needs to align with the human algorithm that is the user experience and the intent. It is basically what a human expects and accordingly fetches possibilities from the platform. Instead of thinking computing, tech giants are designing their algorithms to make them more human-centered and relevant. Even if accounts lose engagement on individual posts, they might still gain more followers and promise an overall better user experience. If this change is implemented rapidly, this might affect your audience engagement. In this case, you will have to follow tactics that will hold your audience's interest and acknowledge individual posts for creativity and originality, while getting familiar with the concept of a human algorithm to reach your desired audience and get more followers.

Using Artificial Intelligence to Filter Out Fake News

One of the main reasons why users do not usually trust social media platforms for current affairs and up-to-date information is the spread of fake news. False information can significantly affect people's sense of perception, and that is why social media giants and developers are relying on artificial intelligence to filter out fake news and segment data to present accurate and reliable information. With an unfathomable amount of content created and posted on social media, people need a utilitarian artificial intelligence system within the algorithm to crack the complex data and clean it for legitimate results.

Changes to Expect from Specific Platforms

Here is how individual social media channels are experimenting with changes and adding features, some of which can be put into use in 2020:

Instagram

- **Hiding the Likes**

Instagram has been testing this new feature of hiding likes from posts in countries such as Italy, Australia, Ireland, and Japan since the year 2019. While hackers and bots are slowly creeping in to increase fake followers and likes, companies and creators who produce genuine content are affected. Also, the new generation is highly affected by the number of likes garnered by their posts and content, which forces them to compare. Eventually, the result is disappointment and self-doubt. To make the user experience more authentic, Instagram is working on hiding likes from posts. You, as the owner of your account and content, can view the number of likes. Depending on the type of discipline you are in, this may or may not affect your marketing strategies. For instance, if you're an entrepreneur, you will need to focus more on your number of followers than your likes. But if you're an influencer, your work and content generation might get somewhat affected.

- **Enhanced Business Tools**

Even though Instagram has massively improved its business tools feature in the past few years, there might be bigger and better changes this year. Many companies are handling business through Instagram now, which is likely why you are here, too. Switching to a business account instead of a personal one gives you additional benefits like insight into user engagement, audience interaction with individual posts, and direct contact with potential customers. This year, you might see improved customer service and tweaked insight statistics, helping you to generate more revenue.

Facebook

• Focus on Groups

Facebook has been working on improving its groups feature for enhanced user experience since 2017. With useful add-ins such as watch party and Facebook pixel, users were able to revamp their content engagement experience. A few additions and design changes made in 2019 also proved to be successful. They drove more people to use this augmented feature and increased interaction. This year, expect a further boost in the groups tab that will pique users' interest, helping your business grow through social media.

• Cryptocurrency and Facebook Pay

Facebook is all set to launch Calibra, its dedicated wallet, to introduce its own global payment system. Facebook's digital currency is called Libra, and it aims to change and dominate the payment discipline around the world. It is designed to be used for normal transactions like paying grocery bills as well, without any transaction costs. Calibra will be integrated into Facebook, Messenger, and WhatsApp. This will majorly affect your methods of carrying out business transactions.

YouTube

• Ads You Cannot Skip

Even though people are currently witnessing this feature that was added at the beginning of 2019, YouTube is aiming to extend this practice because more people are using the application on their smart TVs. This can elevate your streaming experience and give you opportunities to present your content to a bigger audience. With the addition of the TrueView ad unit, you can seamlessly incorporate creativity that was initially targeted to TV viewers.

- **Creation of Original Content**

People have seen YouTube rolling out original content with its own series and live events being streamed on the platform. While there is no Premium paywall on it anymore, the platform might invest more in producing this kind of original content this year. It is also produced with versatility and diversity in mind. It marks the importance of content originality, especially advertisements. You really need to focus on this aspect if you are planning on using YouTube as one of your primary platforms for marketing.

Snapchat

- **Enhanced AR Filters**

Augmented reality is booming in this technology-driven era, with social media platforms keen on passing the experience on to their users. Snapchat has always been—and probably will be—the leading platform to use this tool. With creative tools, interactive templates, and the use of geolocation, Snapchat makes people think, "What's next?"

The platform recently shook hands with a computer vision startup, AI Factory, which will help in enhancing existing features and creating plausible interactive tools. Also, you can expect some goofy AR filters that will probably go viral.

- **Ad Tools**

Snapchat is really stepping up its ad game with the recent introduction of Dynamic Ads. It is still experimenting with updated formats that can be released this year. The feature of Dynamic Ads can be extremely helpful for marketers and content creators trying to sell products or services. These are tweaked to change particular product information and present it in its most creative and truest form. You can choose from a wide range of templates available that work as complete product catalogs for all disciplines and have been successful in catching users' attention. With better ad experiences expected this year, you can fully benefit from this feature by targeting younger users, as they constitute the majority of users.

Twitter

•Switching Accounts in Replies

A probable feature rolling out this year could be the ability to switch accounts while you are replying to a tweet. This could help in replying to potential clients, using both your accounts spontaneously. While this feature was merely an experiment, it is likely to be made permanent this year.

• Tweeting to Specific Topics or Friends

Dantley Davis, the vice president of Twitter's design and research department, recently displayed a list of probable features that could be introduced this year. One of the main highlights was the feature of tweeting to specific subjects, friends, or hashtags. This will allow you to tweet on specific subjects or promote your business in segments by using particular hashtags or targeting your audience group. It is aimed at preventing spamming and targeting users who are truly curious. However, it may also open up the potential of forming private discussions or groups, similar to Facebook. In that case, you will have to channel your strategies in the right direction wisely.

As you can see, many of these foreseeable changes across all social media platforms can benefit your marketing strategies, while a few of them need to be molded and targeted to your advantage. Improved features like refined customer service, more ads across all platforms, and enhanced business and interaction tools can make your business marketing stronger than ever.

Chapter 3: Social Media Trends for 2020

As you start thinking that social media has reached its peak, it tends to do better and prove you wrong. The last five to seven years have witnessed a drastic growth in social media use, with marketers and brands making all these platforms their main base for advertising. If you are just entering this game now, you need to stay ahead of time. While you're already aware of the changes that might occur in social media this year, here are some of the trends that you must follow to stand out and generate more leads.

Trend 1: Powerful Storytelling

The power of authentic advertising was revealed in this past decade, with agencies and brands creating content that oozed creativity and originality. People can anticipate how audiences can be attracted to advertising and marketing that is pure genius.

Here is how you can grab your audience's attention with some remarkable and powerful storytelling:

Personalization

You know your story will hit the mark when the majority of your audience can relate to it. Although considered an underrated tactic, personalization can actually be a game-changer for you. Many marketers are now realizing this and actively using it within their phases of marketing strategies. It not only helps your audience to make a wiser purchase decision but also leaves a great impression on them. You might have noticed how Spotify rolled out personalized statistics for every user at the end of 2019. This was an amazing way to generate more interaction, and Spotify was thoroughly successful in achieving it.

Hitting the Current Affairs

Staying up to date with current news and using it to your advantage is another underrated yet powerful strategy that can be used in a scholarly marketing plan. One great example of a brand that follows smart advertising and uses powerful storytelling, mainly through current affairs, is Burger King. A recent piece of news about Prince Harry and Meghan Markle stepping back from their senior royal roles was seen as a great marketing tactic by the brand. They instantly tweeted, "@ harry, this royal family offers part-time positions" and "You can still eat like a king with us, Harry." While some followers appreciated Burger King for their brilliant timing, others criticized the brand for crossing the line. In both cases, they got enough publicity by gathering more audience engagement that eventually helped their business.

Using Humor

Audiences of all ages can relate to comedy and humor, depending on its context and subject. It is high time you understood the value of humor, too; you can actively use it this year within your content. Two brands that have taken over Twitter and Facebook with their humorous one-liners, clever photo uploads, and witty comebacks are Taco Bell and Old Spice. A recent tiff between Taco Bell and Old Spice on Twitter interested their audiences and significantly increased their engagement. Using humor shows that your brand is authentic, human, and relevant.

Trend 2: Video Content and Engagement

Sure, images and text can be interactive to a certain extent, but video content triumphs in enticing your audience. It creates more interaction and audience engagement. Almost all social media platforms like YouTube (obviously), Facebook, Instagram, Snapchat, and even Twitter have witnessed an exemplary engagement with video content, with more shares, likes, and comments. As a marketer, you need to tap into more video content generation compared to images, especially this year. Instead of reading a long paragraph, users are more interested in learning about your product through a video. With around 81 percent of brands using video content to increase engagement, the upcoming years will generate around 82 percent of online traffic from video content.

If your content was made more interactive and engaging, people would be keener on purchasing your products. Until now, marketers believed that videos with shorter spans could engage audiences more, which is completely going to change from now on. Videos of more than five minutes will engage users due to the emotional connection built midway (depending on the type of content, of course). Also, 360-degree videos will be all the rage among marketers. Tap into it before your competitors know about its potential.

Trend 3: Rise of Influencer Marketing

The rise of social media also witnessed a rise in influencers. It is 2020—people are doing what they love and getting paid for it. Many influencers have found their passion and acknowledged their talent using social media platforms. Numerous beauty, fashion, travel, and food bloggers have risen above their insecurities and built their own community on these platforms. With their increase in popularity, brands are making full use of their audience reach. You might have come across numerous brands and influencers collaborating over a product, which majorly benefits both parties. Influencers are getting hefty paychecks for promotions, especially fashion and beauty bloggers. The preferred media for this practice are Instagram and YouTube.

According to a survey conducted by Hootsuite, 48 percent of their clients used celebrities for promotion, and 45 percent used micro-influencers to reach an audience with a smaller radius but tight engagement.

This year, people can expect a major change among all influencers. More and more bloggers are shifting toward promoting their own brands and blogs instead of promoting other businesses. People can also expect a lot of collaborations, with a few big ones starring numerous top-level influencers for mega engagement. As for marketing agencies, they will probably still set budgets to sponsor influencers that are looking for extra content and weighty paychecks. Basically, there is no stopping influencers in 2020—and for many more years to come.

Trend 4: Stories and IGTV Videos

The previous chapter talked about how stories have been a major hit as a new feature for user engagement. Using this impressive add-in to promote your content promises a huge success this year. While Snapchat had the initial concept of disappearing content, Instagram, Facebook, and WhatsApp incorporated this feature into their networks to improve user experience and increase engagement. Instagram is, however, constantly updating this feature, making it useful for marketing agencies and influencers.

With innovative tools like colorful fonts, art features, filters, stickers, and Boomerangs, stories have been extremely popular, and they are here to stay in 2020 as well. You can cross-promote your posts through stories, or link your website with your stories for more followers. Brands are also developing specific story templates to enhance storytelling and increase engagement with their followers.

Since Instagram videos have a limited watching time, the social media platform introduced a new feature called IGTV videos in 2018 that allowed users to watch content from a minute to an hour. Even though IGTV videos went through a rocky start at first, a few tweaks and updates have given them the significance they deserve. They are now extensively used by content marketers and influencers to promote their products and content. IGTV videos seem to have a bright future this year and beyond. Even though the majority of marketers and influencers still opt for YouTube and Facebook to promote video content, IGTV videos should also be considered. Here are some cool ways you can use IGTV videos to promote your content in 2020:

➤ Create portrait or vertically-formatted content that takes up the entire screen, as it enhances usability.

➤ Use a landscape format to reach a bigger audience.

➤ Use the IGTV preview option to get easily discovered in the "Explore" feed.

➤ Create polls and ask questions about the type of video content your followers like to watch. This will increase interaction, and you'll know what your audience loves.

Trend 5: Increase in Shopping

With more and more brands establishing their names daily, people have a myriad of options and products to shop online. And with the powerful tool of social media, every brand is trying to create its own niche to be recognized. Content marketers and advertisers are trying to build brand awareness and identity to entice more customers into buying their products. All this has led to an increase in sales, and social media alone is generating billions of dollars in revenue for brands every year.

The development and marketing of company websites have been in place for a decade, giving birth to e-commerce. However, with the popularity of social media shopping, social e-commerce is now at its peak, showing a promising future for 2020 as well. So, if you are here to understand how to sell your products or services on social media, you're in luck. The numbers speak for themselves. While more than 50 percent of customers discover and find products on Facebook and Instagram, at least 30 percent of them make purchases through social media platforms.

Chief brands like Nike realized this potential, which led them to use the feature of in-app purchases; they have a dedicated Facebook and Instagram shop. This way, your customer can make a purchase while staying within the app, which helps to generate more sales. Instagram has also recently developed a shopping feature that lets you tag up to five products in a post. You can get additional information about the product when you click on the tag. This feature has let brands generate huge amounts of revenue. With additional helpful elements, such as the "swipe up" feature and plug-ins that create invoices and confirmation, social media platforms are further developing their features to enhance social e-commerce.

Trend 6: Incorporation of Augmented Reality for Customers

Even though augmented reality has already been discussed as a major change that can be expected in 2020, it can also be considered a great trend in marketing strategy. Often confused with virtual reality, augmented reality is the incorporation of real-life scenes into computer-based graphics, designed to improve user experience. While Snapchat has already implemented AR filters and used geolocation as a key feature, other social media platforms are also using augmented reality extensively. You must have played Pokemon Go, which was all the rage among users around the globe a few years ago. You could see Pokemons running around in the real world through your camera lens. As much as people enjoyed this feature, they could not help but think more about this pioneering tech.

As you can see, every platform is increasingly making use of this progressive technological innovation. It is time for you to incorporate it into your marketing strategies as well. You can learn from brands like Sephora and Timberland that are using AR as a marketing strategy. Nike is on its way with a few experiments to provide its customers with an interactive experience. The major benefits of using AR for marketing are standing out, fulfilling the expectations of unique content, and selling products at a faster pace than anticipated due to quicker customer decisions.

Even though Snapchat is largely based on AR at present, Facebook and Instagram are also working toward becoming fully AR-based. Until you are introduced to a new innovation, you can start building your marketing plan around the existing augmented reality features that are available and popular across social media platforms, such as filters, bitmojis, maps, and location tags. Again, it can be advantageous to target younger audiences because millennials and Gen Z make up the majority of these users.

While you definitely need to keep an eye on these strategies, it is a good idea to keep exploring and looking for new options and trends that might just boom anytime in today's world. Whether you are using YouTube, Instagram, Twitter, or Facebook, fill in the gaps using strategies that are directed toward individual social media platforms.

Chapter 4: Personal Branding— Are You Doing It Right?

With the market being completely saturated in many fields, most people find it easier to relate to an individual rather than a company. That is why personal branding makes all the difference. However, when it comes to personal branding, you need to understand how to do it right as it can also negatively impact your business's image or reputation.

To help you figure out if you are on the right track or not, you must first understand the difference between personal branding and product branding.

Product Branding

Each brand represents a specific product or service and should portray a certain image to deliver a message through the product or service at hand, as well as taking into consideration the elements of branding such as design, font, color, logo, and overall vibe. Branding is important because it has the power to make the target audience recognize your products instantly and feel a specific way concerning your brand.

Personal Branding

Personal branding, on the other hand, goes a little further. Instead of focusing just on the product or service that your company offers, it focuses on an individual. A personal brand is all about you as a person and the image you choose to portray to the world. Adding a human touch to any brand makes it easier to connect with and more appealing to customers.

Because this type of branding makes it so much simpler for an audience to relate to a person instead of a product or service, using personal branding can have quite successful effects. If you choose to use this method, here are a few tips to make sure you are doing it right:

Clean Out Your Social Media Platforms

If you choose to put yourself out there and use the image that represents your business as a form of personal branding, you need to ensure that your personal social media platforms also align with the brand identity and do not have any negative impact on your brand. While interacting with a face can be extremely effective when it comes to marketing on social media, it can also backfire if you are not careful with the image you put forward. That is why the first thing you need to do is clean up your social media accounts; delete any images or posts that do not correspond with your brand's identity or values, and be wary of what you share on your social media platforms. Choosing to use personal branding means that your actions also reflect that of your brand.

This does not mean that you cannot post anything personal or need to be professional 100 percent of the time; it just means that you need to think twice about the things you post, the tone of voice you use, your language, and how personal you get with your accounts.

Be Consistent

An essential part of using personal branding on social media is consistency. Not only in the images, vibe, and choice of content you post but also in the values that you represent. Say you are trying to promote sustainability. If you are all about saving the environment and raising awareness of the problems of using plastics, you need to ensure that you do not contradict yourself on your social platforms by collaborating with a brand that is harmful to the environment and produces a whole lot of plastic waste. This will not only infuriate your followers but also put your reputation and credibility—as well as your company's reputation—at risk. When it comes to promoting core values, you need to be consistent or separate your business and personal life.

Maintain a Visually Appealing Front

When representing your brand, your profile is no longer your free space to do whatever you want. On the contrary, it should be treated as an extension of your business with a similar brand identity, but with a greater focus on you. That is why you must use high-quality photographs, instead of those just taken on your phone. You should also use the same color palette and harmonious vibes throughout your page. The important thing is that you make your accounts visually appealing as any potential customer or business partner will check out your accounts first before making a deal with you. They need to be greeted with a positive vibe as soon as they access your accounts.

One of the strongest ways to promote a brand is to identify it from a distance. As a tool for personal branding, you also need to adhere to the same values, content, and overall vibe that make your business unique.

Find the Most Suitable Platform for Your Business

There are many different platforms on social media that cater to not only different age groups but different genders or interests. Since the majority of Internet users are on Facebook, you would think that it would be the best tool for social media marketing and creating your own personal branding account to reach a broader audience. However, you could find that the audience on Facebook is not suitable for your brand and not age-appropriate either. While Facebook focuses on content and news, Instagram is a much better platform for a business that is focused mainly on visuals. It is not enough just to follow the guidelines for personal branding; they will only be effective if used on the right medium, where the audience will be able to interact and communicate with the image you are setting.

Analyze Your Audience

Creating a personal brand allows you to keep an eye on your audience through social media and get closer to them. The more you interact with them, the more you will be able to identify what resonates with them the most. This way, you'll get a better understanding of the changes that can be made to ensure your business's success. You'll also be able to gain insight into who else your audience follows and identify key social media influencers that can be beneficial to your brand. This can lead to potential collaborations or ideas regarding what your target audience will be interested in according to their interaction with your posts.

Choose Other Brand Ambassadors

With personal branding, you do not have to expose yourself or become one with your brand in order to have a shot at succeeding. People like to get a feel of the brand through a person, but it doesn't necessarily have to be you. That is why many companies use brand ambassadors to make them the face of the company as a form of personal branding.

However, when choosing a brand ambassador, basing your decision on numbers is not enough. Because they will be the face and image representing your business, you must make your decisions wisely. They need to be not only a good match in terms of aligning with your brand identity and core values but also a public figure that your target audience appreciates and looks up to. They should want to get to know your business more because they represent it. You need to choose someone who will resort to their social media channels and market your products smoothly, without it putting people off.

In most cases, having a brand ambassador can really help you reach a wider audience as they not only have a high following on their social media platforms but are also influential figures in the community with access to your specific target audience. Using brand ambassadors for personal branding opens up different opportunities and exposes your brand to many different channels that can significantly benefit the business. Just be wise in your choices, as any damage that a brand ambassador may cause could end up harming your image, too.

Be Active on Social Media

Representing your business's image through personal branding means that you need to be active to grow a following and keep the existing audience engaged. The frequency of posts may differ according to each platform you are using, but in general, it is essential to keep your audience coming back for more – meaning that you need to be active daily. The more consistent you are, the more your sales will increase, as many people tend to be skeptical at the beginning. However, they will eventually give in as they keep seeing the product being promoted, not only because this makes it constantly remain at the back of their minds, but also because they start to gain more detailed information and get familiar with the product or service with every post they see. If you are wondering how frequently you should be posting, here is the optimum amount of posts per day for each platform based on Buffer's studies and research:

> • **Facebook** – it is best to post two times per day. It can be split into once in the morning and another time in the evening to suit different people who access Facebook at various times of the day.

- **LinkedIn** – it is recommended that a business only post once per day because many people on LinkedIn are more interested in finding jobs and are busy at work.
- **Twitter** – it is best to grab your audience's attention by posting five times per day because of the small number of characters allowed per tweet.
- **Pinterest** – it is ideal for a business to post five times a day since many people are very active and continuously flicking through different boards.
- **Instagram** – focus on posting strong visuals one and a half times per day. That means you can post two on one day and one the next to space them out.

Another way of being active on social media and promoting successful personal branding content is by engaging with your community as much as possible. This can be done by organizing a local charity, taking part in a marathon in your local area, or even sponsoring a kids' show. This will help you get familiar with the community as well as promoting your personal branding to show that you are giving back and interested in leaving a positive footprint – instead of just selling your products. It will also appeal to people on a personal level and make them trust your brand even more. Besides, it can open up more opportunities for collaborations and make for useful, appealing content for your social media platforms.

Video Content

Video content is really picking up, and your personal branding needs to incorporate that to keep up with the trend. This can be done through Instagram stories, IGTV on Instagram, or your very own YouTube channel. Just make sure that the content is relevant, catchy, short, appealing to your audience, and in line with your personal image. Providing the audience with what they want to see and what competitors in your industry are doing will help make your personal branding more appealing.

Remember that personal branding is a great way to expand your social media presence and help you connect with a wider audience. It is always easier to trust a business with a face, as it helps you understand the core values of the business and be sure that you are in good hands. However, before you go ahead and expose a certain image to the public, you need to analyze the situation and make sure that the person in question will have a positive impact on your business's reputation, rather than possibly harming it in the future.

Chapter 5: Knowing and Growing Your Audience

Social media can be a very effective tool for marketing, but you need to have a strong social media presence. To do that, you need not only to understand your audience and what appeals to them but also who your target audience is, what makes them unique, and how to appeal to a specific niche to give you an advantage.

Pinpointing Your Audience

One of the most difficult—yet crucial—tasks for any business is to specify a target audience and narrow it down to a niche market that will benefit from your business and find your products or services appealing.

Having a specific target market should already be part of your business plan. However, as you start your business, you will be able to make an even better analysis based on those that are interested in your products or services and interact with your posts. This allows you to narrow down your target audience and market to those who are most likely to buy your products. You'll find that the people in your target audience have common characteristics or interests, such as demographics, behaviors, or hobbies.

You must define your business's target audience as clearly as possible because this will help you benefit from targeted advertising, which allows you to be extremely specific. This way, you spend advertising money only on those most likely to be interested in making a purchase. This not only boosts your sales but also makes the return on investment for every dollar spent on marketing worth it. However, an important question you should ask is, "How do I figure out who my target audience is?" It is not enough just to have an idea of who your products would be suitable for; there are ways to find out who will benefit from your business and are part of the target audience you should be addressing.

Characteristics to Help You Define Your Audience

- **Age**

You need to understand which generation you are targeting. This will help you adjust your content accordingly, even in your tone of voice, visuals, and especially your ad campaigns. Age is also a factor in deciding what platform is the most suitable and will generate the most profit because different age groups tend to use different social media platforms. It is not essential to pinpoint a specific age, but just an average range to help you make better decisions when it comes to marketing.

- **Gender**

In some cases, you could find that one gender finds your business more appealing than the other, and knowing this will help you market specific products and posts to them.

- **Location**

One of the advantages of Facebook is that it is a global network that allows you to target anyone in the world. However, if your products or services only cater to a specific location, it's essential to highlight that. This will allow you to consider several factors, such as geographic areas to target for your promotions or advertising. It will also help you determine the time zone of your audience, allowing you to be present when your customers are most likely to be active so that you can answer their questions and provide excellent customer service through engagement and interaction. It's also imperative for you to accommodate the time zone when scheduling your social media posts as well as ad campaigns.

- **Language**

Your target audience may likely be speaking a different language. Say your business provides Middle Eastern desserts in North America. You could find that your target audience speaks Arabic rather than English, and so, it is important to take into account their dominant language.

- **Budget and Spending Habits**

It is beneficial to gather information about the spending patterns of your target audience. This will help you understand how to price your products and whether your budgeting is effective concerning your audience. Understanding how much they are willing to spend on a product, as well as how frequently they buy items within your price range, will help you get a better idea of how you should approach your pricing and how successful your marketing will be with promotions and sales.

- **Interests**

There are numerous advantages in determining the interests of your target market. You can do this by analyzing the people who regularly interact with your posts and figuring out what they have in common. You could find that most of them like yoga pages, or have a sweet tooth, or even like to travel. These interests, no matter how specific, will really come in handy when it is time to target your social media ads to a specific audience, helping you gain a wider reach of suitable users.

All of the above is extremely useful information that will really help your business, but where do you get that information from? And how do you determine all these factors to help you narrow down who your target audience is? It is simple: analytics. Going on each platform and checking out the available insights will not only help you determine who your target audience is but also gain the necessary insight into which platform to use for which target audience.

Growing Your Audience

Once you are familiar with your target market, the next question you should ask is, "How does my target audience know that my business exists?" Being able to reach and grow your audience is essential for your business to succeed. Luckily, social media can really help you grow your audience, as it allows you to target ads at them specifically once you have gained valuable insight into their characteristics and interests.

Set Fixed Goals

Key factors that will help you grow your audience are a set plan and strategy that will enable you to reach specific users according to their habits. For instance, while Facebook remains the most widely used social media platform, the majority of millennials and younger users are usually found on Instagram, Twitter, or Snapchat, making it more effective to channel your advertising there if that is the age range you are interested in. However, if you're looking to grow a specific platform for business purposes, you could still work on targeting them as they tend to access various platforms.

Having a plan will enable you to create content that will help you reach your goals and work on specific targets. If you are familiar with your target audience and have the specific goal of reaching a broader audience on Facebook, then you can go about creating engaging content, addressing your audience, and filtering your targeting options to ensure that your paid reach is beneficial. This can result in more people interacting with your posts, and liking your page, or buying your products.

When setting goals, one of the most common and effective methods is the S-M-A-R-T method, which stands for the following:

➢ **Specific:** Make sure that you have clear, defined goals.

➢ **Measurable:** Set goals that can be measured so that you can analyze your level of success and monitor your achievements.

➢ **Achievable:** Avoid setting impossible goals and make sure that what you aim for can actually be achieved with the resources you have.

➢ **Realistic:** Be realistic about the budget, the expected time frame to achieve your goals and the outcome.

➢ **Time-Sensitive:** Follow a detailed schedule to help you determine how long it would take you to achieve your goals.

Analyze Your Competitors

To stand out, you need to study the market and figure out what your competitors are doing. Once you have analyzed them, you can start identifying the key factors that make their methodology work— what is it that attracts their audience and appeals to them? Answering these questions can help you understand what your business needs to do. You do not necessarily have to copy them, but you do need to understand what their edge is. This way, you will gain more insight into your target audience and work on coming up with a different edge or finding a gap in the market that you can focus on to attract more followers to your business rather than your competitors.

By looking at the content they share, their engagement, and the frequency in which they post, you can create and apply a successful strategy. Choose more relevant content that is more engaging and will appeal better to your target audience. You can analyze your competitors by searching for the probable keywords on each platform.

Create a Brand Voice

There is a certain lingo, tone, and way of speaking that will attract different age groups. So, once you are familiar with your specific target audience, you should start studying how they text, post, and speak, as well as what their interests are to help create a voice for your brand. This will make them feel more encouraged to interact with your posts and build a connection with your business.

You can even use a caption from a trending TV show that this age group watches, or lyrics from a song they listen to when you find it relevant. This will encourage them to engage with your post and therefore help you reach a wider audience.

Enhance Your Reach

There are several factors you need to take into consideration when it comes to reaching a wider audience. From paying for advertisements to posting at the most suitable times that promote the best engagement, you need to make sure that everything you do is verified, studied, and will help you reach that goal.

Here are the best times to post on each platform:

➢ **Facebook:** While 10 a.m. - 3 p.m. on weekdays are usually the safest times to post on Facebook, the most effective time is usually Thursday, between 1 p.m. - 2 p.m.

➢ **Instagram:** Just like Facebook, Thursday is also the best day to post on Instagram, whereas the safest timings for this platform are from Tuesday to Friday between 9 a.m. - 6 p.m.

➢ **Twitter:** The best time to post on Twitter is on Friday, around 9 a.m. - 10 a.m.

➢ **LinkedIn:** Between 3 p.m. - 5 p.m. on Wednesday is the best time to post on this platform.

Scheduling posts for these timings will allow you to capitalize on the most engaging times of each platform and give your posts an extra push to help them reach your target audience, growing it in the process.

Following these proven strategies to identify and grow your target audience will really help boost your sales, strengthen your social media presence, and make your brand look more authentic and appealing to new followers. Once you have figured out who your target audience is and how to appeal to them, the rest is just a piece of cake.

Chapter 6: Which Platform Should You Use?

With the wide range of social media platforms available today, it is understandable to be confused about which one would be the best for your business. After all, there are budget restrictions and tight schedules to adhere to, and you cannot dedicate and distribute equal amounts of your time to every social media platform there is. That would not make any sense, either, because you need to think about your target audience, business type, and goals. Not every platform is meant for you. One of the key factors in successful business marketing is choosing the right platform. And while there are numerous options to choose from, you will now delve into each one to understand what is best for your business this year.

Facebook

Facebook has been thriving for more than a decade now and is undoubtedly one of the best social media platforms to use for marketing a business. It can be beneficial in targeting users between the ages of 25 and 34, with almost an equal balance of gender distribution. Another notable benefit is that most of the users are educated and have a higher income graph, and it can majorly help your business in driving more sales.

When it comes to existing and probable features, Facebook has come a long way in developing tools that are directed toward promotions and business marketing, making it an effective social media platform. It also offers options to post various types of content, such as images, videos, texts, stories, and links, giving you creative flexibility and a blank canvas to promote your business. One of the important factors to consider is Facebook ads. Also known as Marketplace Ads, this feature appears in a sidebar while browsing through the site. You can use this helpful feature by setting budgets and promoting your business to a specific and interested audience. Other useful features for efficient business marketing on Facebook include Facebook contests, sponsored stories, and paid post promotions.

Instagram

Instagram has rapidly climbed the ladder to be ranked as one of the most sought-after social media platforms in 2019. It shows great promise ahead, too. And so, Instagram should definitely be on your list. This platform showcases a great number of users who follow brands and buy from them. Like Facebook, the majority of Instagram's audience also consists of educated people in higher income brackets. This is good news for your business. As for the features, you can use Instagram's business tools that offer direct interaction with your customers and show statistics like user engagement and the number of shares. It allows you to fix your content and promote it the right way to achieve further engagement.

As discussed earlier, Instagram's shopping feature can also come in handy. If your business aims to sell products, Instagram is your best bet, right after Facebook. You can post images, videos, stories, and links within stories to promote your brand and showcase your creativity. If you are thinking of using just two or three social media platforms for marketing, Instagram must be one.

Snapchat

Snapchat has slowly evolved from an entertainment platform into a marketing channel. Many people underestimate the power of

Snapchat in marketing their businesses, but it actually has a lot of potentials. The first benefit is the target audience. As previously pointed out, this social media platform mainly attracts younger audiences, especially Gen Z. If your business aims to sell products or services to teenagers and young adults, Snapchat is the answer. Roughly 71 percent of the Gen Z population uses Snapchat regularly. Your content will successfully reach users between the ages of 12 and 34.

Snapchat uses the concept of stories in the form of images and videos. Even though there is a limit to developing content, you are given the flexibility to post constantly, without going overboard. You have a blank canvas each day, and followers often forget the content that you posted previously as it disappears within 24 hours. One major tactic that brands use on Snapchat is creating sponsored filters, as Snapchat users love playing with filters and lenses. Recently, brands like Taco Bell and Gatorade gained massive interaction by creating their own filters. You can also promote your brand by hiring an influencer who will take over your account for a day.

Twitter

Twitter is all about the power of text in a few characters. The majority of the audience on Twitter tends to be between 18 and 29 years of age, making it a viable option to target a younger audience. Again, the bulk of Twitter's audience is educated and falls under higher income brackets. One of the main concepts that Twitter beholds is the use of hashtags to reach a certain audience group or follow the trending topics on the platform.

Twitter offers the options of posting images, videos, and mainly text to voice your opinion or promote your brand. Since around 7,000 tweets are uploaded every second, your content needs to be powerful to be seen and shared across the platform. Twitter is actually a great way to interact with your audience, and it demands content that drives more engagement. Remember the humorous feud between Taco Bell and Old Spice; it created amazing engagement and promoted the brands.

There is great potential for advertisements on Twitter, too. You can either choose from Twitter's ad format options or promote your brand's tweet to encourage engagement. Another feature that is provided by this platform is Twitter chats, which can be used for maximum interaction and gaining followers.

YouTube

While YouTube is restricted to video content marketing, it can still be used effectively. The scope of video content was mentioned earlier, and YouTube stands true to being a great marketing platform. With around 74 percent of users watching brand-produced content, 90 percent of which watch videos on a smartphone or laptop, YouTube offers great potential to reach a massive audience. It is one of the biggest platforms that have a major influencer impact. Numbers show that more than 50 percent of users have reacted positively to the content and responded well to the products displayed.

With no limit to uploading content, you can stretch your video's content according to the engagement it receives. You can also link or share your video to other social media platforms, increasing the quality of your content presentation. Use call-to-action tools to increase engagement, such as linking your Facebook or Instagram accounts, requesting subscriptions, likes, and shares, and providing a direct path to your blog or website. YouTube also provides you with a big SEO benefit, as Google can directly display a path to your YouTube video if the keywords match.

TikTok

TikTok is a great platform for content creators who are just starting out and want instant recognition. You will find the majority of the Gen Z audience on this recently viral social media platform. Following the same concept of stories and IGTV videos that last from nine to 15 seconds, TikTok has attracted around 500 million users around the world. It is still debatable whether or not it's the right platform for marketing your business, however.

If you are planning to keep your brand identity subtle and composed, TikTok is not for you. It is rather rushed and wacky. If you want some humor and creativity to be continuously incorporated into your content, this platform can help you with it. You can either show the features of your products or create a few short "how-to" videos instead of creating memes that could backfire on your marketing strategy. For instance, the cosmetic brand Lush regularly uploads videos showing the making of their products, which garners attention. You can also collaborate with TikTok influencers who have a massive impact on their audiences. Before taking action, you should discover the platform more and make an informed decision.

LinkedIn

Leaning more toward the professional side, LinkedIn can connect you with potential partners or customers. If you plan to start a business that requires professional connections, and you are willing to hire employees, LinkedIn is the right platform for you. You can constantly post findings, studies, demographics, or milestones achieved by your company, which will be seen on the main feeds of your connections. With 32 percent of users having acquired a degree and 24 percent holding certifications, the bulk of your audience on LinkedIn will fall under average or higher income brackets.

It is a great platform to generate B2B leads and create ads that promote brand awareness. You can also send personalized messages to your followers or audience when they are active to boost interaction. LinkedIn also has influencers and executives that can create a huge impact on the targeted audience. Even if your brand or business does not possess a corporate identity, you can still use LinkedIn as a plausible tool for gaining your audience's attention.

Pinterest

If the majority of your marketing strategy is based on image branding, Pinterest is the right platform for you. This social media platform acts as a brochure of images that target all disciplines, from art to fitness, and from home decoration to fashion advice. It attracts audiences based on aesthetics. A large part of Pinterest's audience is women (around 79.5 percent), who tend to browse the platform for various purposes. A chief factor that can be converted into an advantage is that you can find people from all age groups on Pinterest, mainly between the ages of 18 and 65, most of whom are educated. If you own a women-centric brand, especially if it targets mothers or women who are expecting, you must tap into Pinterest. Almost eight out of ten moms use Pinterest in the United States, which can be a significant benefit.

You can use a Pinterest business account, connect your other social media accounts to it, claim your website, put in contact details for customers to get in touch with you and create your board. Pinterest also allows for advertising and inserting links to your pins. Use the analytics tool to learn more about popular pins and to get more interaction. Produce your content in a vertical frame range to suit the Pinterest layout and to make it more aesthetically pleasing.

These social media platforms can be—and commonly are—used for effective business marketing. Now, that does not mean you should use them all. As a marketer, you definitely need to tap into Facebook, Instagram, Snapchat, YouTube, and Twitter, among other platforms, as these show a lot of promise this year and beyond. Depending on the type of business and content, you need to measure the potential that each platform will offer. If you do not feel the need, don't waste your time signing up for all these platforms, as that will take a toll on your budget and the quality of your content. Instead, focus on just two or three platforms if you are just starting out, and gradually build on that once you have established a dedicated audience.

Chapter 7: Facebook Marketing

Facebook remains the most widely used social media platform and therefore is essential for most businesses regarding marketing on social media. According to Pew Internet's statistics, roughly two-thirds of American adults use Facebook regularly. That accounts for almost 68 percent, making it an excellent medium to use for adults, as most people are already frequent users.

However, for marketing on Facebook to be effective, there are many factors you need to understand and take into consideration to ensure that you are doing it right. That is why you must know what strategies to follow to improve your Facebook marketing and get the most out of a medium that is widely spread and actually quite cheap to advertise on. To do that, here are a few strategies:

Strategy 1: Engaging Content

One of the first things you need to understand is Facebook's algorithm. The idea behind it—and the reason why it is extremely beneficial—is based on hiding boring content. Because the platform is designed to keep people on it for as long as possible, Facebook has a way of only making interesting or successful content visible to its users. The question is: "How does Facebook make this decision, or label something as boring content?" It's pretty simple. Facebook analyzes the content and classifies it according to the engagement on the post. This means that if the post has likes, comments, or shares, it will be considered interesting, and Facebook will allow it to be seen by many users. However, if a post does not generate any engagement, then

Facebook will automatically hide it from users and classify it under boring content. What does this tell us? For your business's posts to be seen, you need to create engaging content for your users.

One of the key aspects that makes Facebook unique and adds an advantage to any business is that Facebook does not just hide boring content, but does the exact opposite if it determines your content is attention-grabbing. That means, if your posts are getting organic interaction, Facebook will give them an extra push by making them visible to more people. That is why any business needs to try and capitalize on that feature by creating the sort of content that will not only appeal to their target audience but will also start a conversation and make them feel the need to comment or share on their own feed.

You would be surprised to know that comments make a huge difference when it comes to recognizing engagement and affecting your post's visibility. The longer the comment, the better, and the more visible your post will be to other users. So, how can you use this information and apply it to your business?

Create Content That Generates an Emotional Response

With the number of photos uploaded on Facebook reaching a staggering 350 million each day, you need to ensure what you are offering is not just like everybody else. That is why the best way of making the users notice your posts is by introducing content that generates emotion. Whether it makes them laugh or cry, fills their heart with warmth, or even provokes them, you need to be able to push a button to get them to interact with your post. Sometimes, it's enough just to make them smile, and you will find them tagging their friends and liking or sharing the post, giving it the opportunity to be more widely spread. So, when you decide to boost it, Facebook will help it reach a wider audience, making your marketing effective at an even lower cost per viewer.

Before you post any content on Facebook or think of what you'll be sharing next on your business's page, ask yourself what kind of emotion it generates. If it looks like it won't trigger an emotion, then find something that will instead.

Use Trending Content to Your Advantage

Being timely not only makes your content relatable but also encourages people to interact and engage with your post as it is something that is happening in the now. Because most people are on Facebook regularly, they tend to get their information from there. So, when a business manages to capitalize on a trend, it instantly gains the attention of the users. Take, for example, the fires in Australia that destroyed thousands of acres of land and a large amount of wildlife. As it was happening, photos of injured koalas and kangaroos were being shared excessively, as this kind of content contains both factors, generating an emotional response, and being timely.

As a business, you could use this to your advantage by either sending a percentage of your proceeds to help those in need in Australia or just writing an emotional post showing the human side of your business. Capitalizing on trending content is a great tool that offers instant rewards and results when it comes to Facebook marketing.

Strategy 2: Video Content

While the rise in video content has already been visible throughout the past couple of years, in 2020, it is expected to increase even more. That is why it's time to resort to videos if you haven't started already. However, there is a specific strategy you need to follow in order to reach your audience and ensure success. Why are videos more effective when it comes to Facebook marketing? Because they get WAY more engagement than photos and text put together! The difference in numbers is not only astounding but also makes it absolutely vital for a business to make use of the effect of videos.

However, most businesses tend to make the mistake of producing promotional or advertorial video content without first building a relationship with their customers. This can make them uninterested in viewing the promotional video you have uploaded, as they are probably unprepared for it. So, how do you get them interested?

There is a proven strategy to help develop a relationship and build rapport with your audience first, in order to make video content effective. This is done by using the 3x3 video strategy of "why", "how", and "what" videos. In this technique, you first build a portfolio of videos that help introduce you as a person and your business idea, along with videos explaining what your process looks like. This can be created in the form of "how-to" videos that will appeal to your audience before introducing the "why" videos, which will be presenting why your products are unique or would benefit the user.

"Why" Videos

As a marketer, you can use the "why" videos to really help your audience connect with your business on a personal level. It is a form of personal branding that allows the user to identify the face behind the business and get to know the backstory. Through this process, you will summarize your story and explain the reason you created your business. It is a simple "why" serving to put your idea across and familiarize people with you and your business. It's essential to start with this step to build successful video content. Think of questions like the following:

➢ What motivated you to start?

➢ What are you known for?

➢ What are you most proud of?

➢ What problems did you face?

➢ What was missing in the market?

In this category, you should start out with three different videos of about 20 to 90 seconds, explaining who you are and the story behind your business. When producing the videos, you should try and focus on reaching a different target audience each time, as you might later notice that one video was more appealing to men, while another was more appealing to women.

"How" Videos

For your next set of three videos, you should present a series of "how" or "how-to" videos. In these, you get the chance to explain the entire process your business goes through to come up with the final product—your audience will hopefully appreciate the work and effort that goes into it. "How to" videos are popular to such an extent that 51 percent of the traffic on YouTube comes from them. While it is a different platform with a slightly different audience, it goes to show just how important it is for your business to produce "how-to" videos.

In this category, you should produce three different videos, each with a different story. Your first video in the "how" series can emphasize explaining how your products come to life, from an initial idea to a final product. It will help your audience have a deeper understanding of how unique your products are, while also getting to know you and your business.

You can further use "how-to" videos to provide your customers with tips and give them some information they can use to create simpler versions of your products at home or even something that can go with your products. For example, if your business is selling ceramic bowls or dishes, your "how-to" series can focus on tips to take into consideration while cleaning the plates or heating them, or even possibly an easy recipe using the plates. You can get creative and see what resonates the most with your audience.

"What" Videos

In this section, you will already have created a relationship with your customers that allows you to start promoting your products. Now is the time to post videos to help you promote the products' unique selling points. In these videos, you can make the audience feel the need to purchase your products.

The "why", "how", and "what" videos are great to get you started on your video content journey on Facebook. However, there are some other aspects you need to consider while you are putting this method into practice.

Additional Tips

- **Only Spend Money on Effective Videos**

Many businesses make the mistake of spending money trying to boost videos that do not appeal to the audience. However, when it comes to video content, the average amount you should be spending is $8-10 for every 1,000 views. If you invest $8 and you only get 500 views or less, then this should be an indication that you need to stop spending more money on your video. That money will be going to waste due to a problem in the content itself, and Facebook is classifying it as "boring".

- **Facebook Video Content Strategy is a Long-Term Plan**

This process could take from six to 12 months. With video content, understanding your audience will take time, so it is important to have patience. During this time, you should know that one out of ten videos will work, meaning that 90 percent of your videos will not. If you need to have ten successful videos, you need to create 100 videos until you get them right.

- **The Ideal Duration is Between 20 and 90 Seconds**

The sweet spot usually hits at the 60th second. Take that into consideration when producing your video content, and try not to make it too long or too short.

- **Monitor Your ThruPlay**

ThruPlay can help you analyze how effective your videos are. It is an optimization and billing tool option for video ads that help you understand whether your video is worth boosting or not. ThruPlay yields the ideal results when it's played until the end or at least for 15 seconds.

- **Test Your Videos on Different Audiences**

Analyze your videos after a week to understand who should be your target audience and cater to them accordingly.

Strategy 3: Facebook Ads

71 billion dollars is spent on TV ads that nobody watches. While the viewership of television has already gone down immensely, those who do still watch tend to hit the mute button when it is time for commercials or to get a snack, go to the bathroom, or do anything else except actually watch the commercial on the screen. So, why do

businesses still resort to paying large sums of money to use an advertising technique that is no longer effective? Ask yourself a simple question to understand just how useless ads have become: "How many times have I clicked on the 'Skip Ad' option that appears on the screen when watching a video?" Most people have never watched a single ad, making it a huge waste of money.

On the other hand, Facebook ads are not only extremely cheap in comparison to the market, but are also very effective to reach a wider audience and grow a business's presence online. However, with Facebook's algorithm constantly changing, you can find yourself spending large sums of money on content that is not effective. To help you have a better understanding of the best way to use Facebook ads to your advantage, here are some key factors you should understand:

Types of Facebook Ads

As a marketer or business owner, the first thing you should understand is what type of ads you could use.

- **Image Ads**

This type of advertisement is one of the simplest and easiest ways to start advertising on Facebook. This is done by choosing to promote one of the images that you have already shared to your Facebook page by boosting an existing post.

- **Video Ads**

Because video is a key marketing tool, video advertising is another way you can choose to use Facebook marketing to your advantage. Your boosted videos can appear on your audience's feeds or on Facebook stories when they have a shorter duration. You can even consider using GIFs or animation in your video content instead of live videos.

- **Video Poll Ads**

While it is only available on mobile devices, this type of Facebook ad requires the audience to become more interactive, making it a tool to increase brand awareness.

- **Carousel Ads**

With carousel ads, your business can highlight different products or services, or even use them to shed light on unique benefits or advantages of a specific product. This is because carousel ads allow you to use up to ten images or videos together.

- **Slideshow Ads**

A slideshow ad puts together a series of still photos, text, or videos from your feed and creates a short video ad. It is a useful tool to showcase a variety of products or services your business offers.

- **Collection Ads**

Another tool designed specifically for mobile devices, this option allows you to put together up to five products that customers can click on to buy, making it an extremely effective tool as it is a direct selling opportunity on Facebook.

- **Lead Ads**

Also designed for mobile devices, this tool allows you to gather information quickly from the users without much typing. This can be used to collect contact info for a newsletter or product trial, in addition to easily receiving questions or feedback.

- **Dynamic Ads**

Dynamic ads are used to help you target users who are already interested in your products but have not made a purchase yet. This type of ad appears on their Facebook feeds, featuring a specific product they have previously searched about or added to their carts. This gives them an extra nudge to make the purchase.

- **Messenger Ads**

With the huge number of people using Facebook Messenger as a texting app, Messenger ads give you access to 1.3 billion people every month. All you have to do is choose Messenger as the desired placement for your ad, and it will only be visible to people using Messenger.

- **Story Ads**

The launch of Facebook stories created another avenue to promote an ad or small video and reach your audience faster. When users access stories, they are already in the right mood to watch whatever comes their way, making it a good time to market your products.

How to Advertise on Facebook

If you already have a Facebook page for your business, then you can follow these steps to create successful ads using Facebook Ads Manager:

- **Step 1: Choose the Objective of Your Advertisement**

One of the great things about Facebook ads is that they offer a variety of marketing objectives for you to choose from to help you optimize your ads and get the best results. To select one that is appropriate for your business needs, you can log into Facebook Ads Manager, click on the Campaigns tab, then select Create to start a new campaign. You will find 11 different marketing objectives, such as brand awareness, reach, traffic, and many others to choose from based on the objective you need for your business.

- **Step 2: Find a Suitable Title for Your Campaign**

The next step is to name your ad campaign to monitor it on the Facebook Ads Manager. In this step, you will also be able to choose the focus of the posts and decide whether you want to highlight post engagement, page likes, or event responses.

- **Step 3: Enter Ad Account Details**

To get your ads up and running, you need to set up your ad account by entering key information. Click on Set Up Ad Account and fill in the necessary details such as country, currency, and time zone.

- **Step 4: Target the Right Audience**

One of the advantages of Facebook as a marketing platform is that it allows you to focus on specific criteria in targeting your audience, unlike any other platform. To start choosing the target audience for your ads, open your Facebook ad campaign, and choose which page to promote. Then, scroll down until you find the option that allows you to add a custom audience of people who are already familiar with your business.

The next step is to choose your target location, age, gender, and language. As you add more optimizations, the approximate reach indicator displayed on the right side of the screen will work more accurately.

To increase the return on investment, you need to use detailed targeting to reach the correct target audience.

➢ Detailed Targeting: In this field, you'll be able to decide whom to target based on demographics, interests, and behaviors. This is where you can get really specific and choose to target people who follow bridal stores, for example.

➢ Connections: You can either choose to target your audience or someone who has interacted with your page before, or choose to exclude them entirely to reach new audiences by selecting Exclude people who like your page. However, if your main focus will be your existing audience, then you can select People who like your page.

- **Step 5: Choose Where Your Ad Will Appear**

The next step is to decide where your ads will show. There is an option that allows your ads to appear on Facebook, Instagram, and Messenger, allowing you to get through to a different audience on several platforms by using the Automatic Placements option. However, you could also choose to specify a type of device, platform, or placement, such as feeds, stories, messages, or even articles.

- **Step 6: Budgeting**

Once you have a fixed budget set, it is time to decide how to allocate that money to the Facebook ad campaign. You can select a daily or lifetime budget and decide on the start and end dates. Then, you decide whether you want the ad to go live straight away or schedule it for a time in the future. Keep in mind that you can choose an optional cost and bid control to ensure you do not go over budget, as there is a cap in place per action rather than for the overall campaign.

- **Step 7: Create Your Ad**

After choosing your ad format based on your objectives, you can use the preview tool at the bottom of the page to get an idea of how your ad will appear in different placements. Once you are satisfied, you can click the green Confirm button to submit the order and then wait for an email confirmation from Facebook to notify you of the ad approval.

Facebook ads are becoming a cheap alternative to many other types of advertising, and they are much more effective. That is why your business must understand how to make the most of Facebook advertising and capitalize on it while it's still relatively cheap. With these tools and tips, you will have a basic understanding of how your business can benefit from Facebook marketing.

Chapter 8: YouTube Marketing

Now that you have learned about Facebook marketing, it is time to delve into another popular social media platform. After hearing enough praise about YouTube being an effective marketing platform, you have to include it in your plan if you haven't yet. This chapter talks about how you can use YouTube to extensively promote your brand, mentioning three optimum strategies and additional tips to execute to achieve success.

Apart from being one of the top social media platforms, YouTube is also the second-largest search engine, following Google. It was mentioned earlier how video marketing is more effective compared to image and text marketing. With YouTube generating 300 to 400 hours of videos every hour, and with a billion daily users, there is no reason for you not to use this platform.

However, building your community and brand awareness can be difficult due to millions of channels that are collectively thriving on this platform. There is so much competition that building your niche and getting recognized could be a major task. To help you overcome these challenges and promote effective brand awareness and engagement, here are a few strategies to use in YouTube marketing this year.

Strategy 1: Optimized Content

Content is king. It is what will attract a broader audience and create more engagement on your channel, helping you grow your brand. Optimizing and tweaking your content to gain more interaction and followers is the number one strategy toward effective marketing. Here is how you can optimize your content for this purpose.

Make a Content Plan

To create an effective content plan, you need to know and follow these three guiding principles:

- **Discover Your Audience**

Even though this has been extensively talked about, this point is restricted solely to YouTube marketing. Once you know your brand, you will know the age group and gender of your target audience. Do some research into the type of videos that they currently watch and their behavior on this platform.

- **Know and Study Your Competition**

You know what they say: "Keep your friends close and your enemies closer." Well, you don't exactly have enemies here because it is all about healthy competition. Knowing about brands and companies within your discipline and the marketing strategies they use can be beneficial. You can watch their videos and point out mistakes or problems that you can avoid in order to improve your content.

- **Set Goals**

Why are you doing this? What is your main objective? Is it to sell more products? Is it to drive more engagement? Ask yourself questions, and set your ultimate goals accordingly. It will give you a clear idea of the right direction toward producing optimum content.

Type of Content

Now that you have created an effective content plan, it is time to explore the types of content that you could use for your brand's marketing. It will, of course, majorly depend on whether you want to sell your products or simply generate more views and interaction. It'll also depend on your target audience and what they prefer to watch, as pointed out earlier. Whether you are managing a fashion brand or opening a food and beverage company, you need to understand your brand and the type of content that'll attract more people to it. Any content created without a purpose or concrete intent is bound to fail.

There are many types of content that bloggers—or in this case, vloggers—use to gain more followers. If you are confused about where to start, you can choose from the existing types that are highly preferred by viewers, such as product reviews, unboxing videos, DIY projects, educational videos, comedy, and "how-to" videos, among several others. These are extremely popular and successful in garnering attention. Or you can experiment with a certain type of content and come up with your own style. It will help your brand stand out and be easily recognized.

Practice Consistency

It is really important to upload content consistently, and this applies to all social media platforms. Now, by consistency, this does not just mean uploading videos regularly; it is rather about uploading a certain type of content that follows a pattern. You must have heard about being consistent multiple times, but what most people don't tell you is how to do it, which is exactly what this book is about. But before the "how", you need to know "why". The answer is that consistency keeps your followers excited and gives them a purpose. It raises expectations that are fulfilled by your videos constantly. Also, YouTube is designed with an algorithm that spreads your content to a bigger audience if you post consistently.

As for the "how", you can start by maintaining an upload schedule—a realistic one. You cannot simply set the goal of uploading a video every two days when you need at least three to four days to shoot and edit it. Prepare a plausible schedule and stick to it. You can set templates for your videos and fix certain factors, such as the fonts and editing type, to keep things flowing. Depending on your content, you can also shoot a long video beforehand and split it into three or four parts to have content for the following days.

Use SEO for Video Titles and Descriptions

It has been mentioned how search engine optimization can affect the discovery of your videos. Because YouTube is a search engine, you can use SEO on this platform to rank your videos higher than others within the same niche. SEO is basically when you insert certain keywords, mostly words or phrases, into your video titles and descriptions based on the common words searched by users. Make sure that they are relevant to your content. You can also add them to your closed captions or subtitles. However, you cannot use all the keywords within your title; it will just make it sound nonsensical. This is where tags come in handy; you can put around ten to 20 tags below every video, which is where you can add those keywords for further search optimization.

And when it comes to captions, since YouTube automatically generates most of the captions, there are high chances of them being inaccurate. You can fix this by adding your own closed captions. This will allow you to add your preferred keywords and present the right information to your audience. You should also consider translating your video into other languages to engage audiences worldwide. This way, YouTube will rank your video higher due to keywords in other languages.

Strategy 2: YouTube Stories

Following in the footsteps of Snapchat, Instagram, Facebook, and WhatsApp, YouTube has also introduced the feature of stories for channels that have 10,000 or more subscribers. YouTube Stories was launched in 2018, and since then, it has offered an additional benefit to the channels and influencers to stay further updated with their subscribers. It looks promising this year, as well.

Stories are commonly viewed as a major engagement tool now, with one-third of the total viewers watching stories and content produced by small and big brands. Companies are actively using the concept of stories and making it an integral part of their advertising plan. The key is to stand out. It all comes down to how well you use this feature, and whether you get the maximum benefit out of it.

Now that the overall importance of stories is clearer, it is time to delve into a few aspects of YouTube Stories to understand it better.

Benefits of using YouTube Stories

Even though it is not an original concept, YouTube Stories offers its own set of benefits due to a few differences and extra features. Here are four amazing ways you can benefit from using YouTube Stories for your content marketing:

- **They Remain on The Feed for Seven Days**

Earlier known as YouTube Reels, these stories stay on your feed for a week, unlike Snapchat, Instagram, and Facebook stories that disappear within 24 hours. It is a major benefit as you can create a compelling storytelling background that lasts for days, and it can be viewed by your potential subscribers days after your upload. Your followers can also view it the next day in case they missed some important content. You can mold your content according to the number of days available. It also keeps your audience aware of your content.

- **They Reach Potential Subscribers**

These also target and engage users who have not subscribed to your channel yet, allowing you to increase your followers. It is a great peek-a-boo strategy to use in triggering curiosity among your present and future subscribers. Even if you are not a subscriber, you can view the stories of other channels and influencers that are trending right on your home page.

- **They Open Up New Opportunities**

Stories are a bonus to every content marketer these days, especially this year. They make for light-weight content, are easy to create, and have a heavy impact on interaction with users. Since YouTube's main concept is based on video content, stories are specifically useful for this platform. YouTube also gives you the flexibility to unleash your creativity with its tools, such as font types, filters, stickers, music, and much more.

- **They Are Simple and Practical**

Stories can be images or video-formatted content that can either contain plain text or simple pictures of your products. You can also use a few snippets from your video, without putting any extra effort to shoot content for your stories.

Through YouTube Stories, you, as a marketer or content creator, will have the opportunity to create extremely light content as opposed to the heavy shots and edited videos that you usually upload. Other great ideas for stories can be behind-the-scenes footage, random and fun interviews with your team members, handing over your stories to an influencer, product reviews, or "how-to" video content like tutorials, discount announcements or giveaways, or a sneak peek of your upcoming campaigns. This is the perfect way to create humorous, entertaining, and engaging content.

Impact on Users

Users are much more open to viewing stories than long heavy videos of more than four to five minutes. Since the average attention span of the majority of users is usually short, stories are the perfect way to capture their attention. So much so that around 63 percent of Instagram and Snapchat users view stories. Around 70 percent of those are American, the majority of which falls under the millennial and Gen Z generations.

YouTube Stories have been perceived more as entertaining content rather than informative guides. They have had an emotional effect on users, grabbing their complete attention—most users stated that they were entirely invested and were "looking for more." Your stories do not need to be perfect, heavily edited, or "staged"; they are ideal for creating a more authentic image of your brand and showing your audience the real scenario.

Creating Stories and Garnering Responses

YouTube Stories can be viewed on the front page of the app, with the highlight being the user's profile picture. You just need to click the Create button, followed by Story. Press the capture button to take pictures or hold it to shoot videos. Edit your content using a wide range of available text options, stickers, and music. You can also directly upload a picture or a video from your phone gallery.

Users can also react and comment on your stories and others' comments with a thumbs up, thumbs down, or a heart icon. You can reply to your followers' comments with images or videos, making it more interactive. However, it would have been more successful if you were provided with a "swipe up" option to link your website to your stories like on Instagram.

What Does its Future Look Like?

While Snapchat and Instagram have been successful in introducing the stories feature, YouTube still has some catching up to do regarding other social media platforms. A few users and critics lashed out at YouTube for adding in the already-overused concept of stories. A few channels and influencers were also upset about the limitation of getting to use the feature only after gathering a community of 10,000 subscribers, which can prove to be difficult on a highly competitive platform like YouTube.

While smaller channels and brands would have to struggle their way toward growth, the already-established channels will gather more followers by using the stories feature. However, if YouTube works on a few issues like opening the option of stories to smaller brands, replying to comments with text, and linking websites with the "swipe up" feature, among others, it is bound to succeed in the coming years.

Strategy 3: YouTube Advertising

YouTube ads are undeniably the best way to promote and sell your products, mainly due to the power of video content. Even if you have developed a stellar video campaign, it is worthless if it does not reach a massive audience. This is where YouTube ads can help. You might have come across ads related to specific products or services that you've recently searched for. When the video content relates to the product you desire, you are bound to watch the entire video for more knowledge. This is how YouTube ads work; by targeting specific keywords and searches.

Types of YouTube Ads

There are three types of YouTube ads to choose for your business:

- **TrueView Ads**

The skippable ads that you see at the beginning of any video are known as TrueView ads. While they are flexible and allow you to experiment with your type of content, they also allow the viewers to use the call-to-action button, increasing the interaction. A major benefit of TrueView ads is that you do not pay for the ad unless your viewer has watched more than 30 seconds of it, or used the call-to-action button. This saves you money on viewers who aren't genuinely interested.

- **Pre-Roll or Non-Skippable Ads**

Running anywhere between 15 and 20 seconds, pre-roll ads are non-skippable ads that appear before the main video starts playing, or in the middle of long videos (also known as mid-roll ads). They were extremely annoying when they were first introduced, but viewers have now gotten used to them. Your company can benefit from these as you have the maximum potential to create a commercialized and focused ad for the interested viewers who will watch the entire video ad. Following a pay-per-click concept for payment, this method offers a suitable space for your ad. This type of ad also includes a call-to-action button for the interested viewers.

● **Bumper Ads**

Typically lasting for six seconds, bumper ads are optimized for mobile phones and are the shortest option for delivering important content. These are non-skippable as well, but much more tolerable due to their shorter duration. Acting as "highlights" or reminders of important products, events, or launches, bumper ads are seen at the end of the main videos. Similar to YouTube Stories, you can either show glimpses of the next launch, sneak peeks of your new products, or a piece of exciting news related to your business.

As powerful as YouTube marketing may be, do not forget to promote your content across various social media platforms. That is the only way to be seen and recognized among millions of other brands. Hire YouTube influencers that have a large fan base to present your business creatively, or opt for cross-promotion. YouTube is a great way to promote your business, and you should start posting the right content and being consistent on your channel as soon as possible.

Chapter 9: Twitter Marketing

A few years ago, using Twitter as a marketing platform was off the charts. However, as time passed, content creators and marketers realized the importance of Twitter, which allowed them to interact directly with their customers, use images and visuals to create authenticity, and present their brand as human. Basically, Twitter allowed all brands and companies to present their raw image to the world, helping in building emotional connections and driving more attention to them. So, it grew as an important marketing platform over the years.

Twitter has, in fact, boomed so much that a few brands use this platform as their primary tool for marketing. And it is suggested that you include it in your main marketing platforms as well. Do not worry if you are just starting out; this chapter details some tips and strategies to help you sail your Twitter boat and be recognized easily within the saturated market.

First, to prepare the strategies that you will be defining for successful campaigns, a few of these tips can help you effectively plan and follow the framed strategies. Even though some of these were discussed earlier, some are necessary to be revised for a favorable outcome in the context of Twitter marketing.

Setting Targets and an Ultimate Goal

To frame a set of targets, you need to ask yourself a few questions: "What's the main objective of launching my brand on Twitter? Do I want to generate revenue by sales? Or do I simply want to create a brand image?" You can also use this platform to increase your customers' loyalty and improve your customer service. You need to list all the reasons and objectives that you are expecting from all campaigns, which will help you in generating content accordingly. It will help you form a clear marketing plan and aim directly at your main goal.

So, once you have defined your targets and started following a solid plan, you can track your progress and keep an eye on your team's performance. Your company will be setting a budget for social media marketing, and it is your job to create a realistic plan and set the strategies that will produce the targeted return on investment.

Number of Accounts

Whether your company consists of a bunch of people just starting out or it is a multifaceted company that has many departments, you need to think about the number of accounts that will be up and running. If you already have a Twitter account with a certain number of followers, that shows great potential—it's recommended that you turn it into a business account for your company. Consider the departments or separate teams within your company and think about whether having separate accounts would be more effective or not.

Planning Your Content

To plan your content and build a specific style, you need to know what your target audience wants. You know how important it is by now because it has been emphasized throughout the book. It paves a clear path for the type of content you want to create, and the pattern that will attract your followers. It is also important to analyze your competition and know the type of content they are posting. You surely want to stand out and create your own identity within the market.

Four Great Ways of Planning

- *Live Video Tweets*

You know the importance of video content marketing and how users are more attracted to this kind of content. A few years ago, Twitter, like other social media platforms, introduced the live video feature, which has been quite successful. You can use this to show behind-the-scenes footage of your business and increase interaction with your followers. Around 80 percent of users tend to remember the videos they watch online. This is a real-time strategy that works wonders for marketing your brand. Your followers have the opportunity to catch a glimpse of the faces behind your brand, and this curiosity drives further engagement.

- *Threaded Tweets*

At times, your marketing plan will be saturated with short tweets and videos. This is when threaded tweets can make a difference. Connecting threads to your tweets increase curiosity among your followers and lets you tell a story instead of limiting it to a few characters. It is now easy for you to share a product review, inform your followers about a launch or event in detail, or simply create an irresistible storytelling tactic. This feature allows you to add more text to further threads once the original tweet is published.

- *Highlighting Social Causes*

If your brand supports a particular social cause, it is necessary to keep it highlighted within your content all the time. From wars to climate change, there is always an ongoing concern or issue around the world. As a global channel, you need to show your concern and take a stand against such issues—your followers will expect nothing less. Once you have established a massive channel, you have the power of reaching millions of people simultaneously and creating major awareness. This will not only help in connecting your brand with like-minded people but also in making your channel stand out by creating a lot of engagement. The "Tweet for a Cause" hashtag has been popular on the platform, and rightly so.

Whenever a major social, cultural, or political issue arises, the "Twitterati" are the ones who respond the fastest. People see many debates and concerns being voiced by people of various nationalities and backgrounds through their tweets. You should consider this neglected factor and use it to your advantage.

- *Marking Important Events or Days*

People around the world celebrate special occasions, festivals, and events that are either globally dominant or are specific to a particular country or community. Marking these events on your calendar and producing content accordingly can help in creating more audience engagement. For instance, India celebrates Diwali, which is an important festival for the country. Creating content that revolves around Diwali and your brand image can garner a lot of attention from India, helping you gain plenty of followers—and probably an increase in sales—due to its massive population.

Another example of an event that reflected on Twitter was the Golden Globes in 2018. The hashtag "2018#GoldenGlobes" went viral, which was followed by numerous relevant tweets. You just need to keep an eye on the calendar and look for events within your region and around the world. It can be anything related to music, festivals, sports, fashion, movies, etc. Try to attend as many events as you can, especially if they are relevant to your brand. Live-tweet while you are there, or take as many photos as you can. Just pay attention to the happenings around you to stay updated.

These methods of creating engagement can surely be helpful, but three specific strategies can help your brand have an edge and lead to massive interaction with your audience—and which are often ignored by other accounts:

Strategy 1: Personalized Responses

Providing your followers with personal responses, no matter which channel they are using, is a great way of gaining their trust and increasing overall interaction. It proves that there are human operators behind your brand, which can play a major role in building an approachable brand image.

Using Sarcasm and Humor

Again, people know how sarcasm and humor can win over a massive number of users. You can use it to show a lighter side of your brand. There are many funny GIFs available online that can be used to prove your point without offending customers and followers. Being consistent in portraying clever humor keeps your followers waiting for more content and responses from your end.

A few examples of brands that consistently use wit within their content and responses are Netflix, KFC, Oreo, and Moosejaw. These brands know how to keep their content original and fresh, as well as keep their fans entertained with clever responses. You can take a more in-depth look at these brands and their marketing strategies to learn more.

However, the stats show that 88 percent of followers dislike sarcastic responses to their inquiries, and feel like brands are mocking them. This could lead to the downfall of you and your brand name, so it is better to avoid using humor if you do not have an aptitude for it. Even if your post goes viral, it could lead to many negative responses instead of positive ones. In this case, it's wiser to avoid the banter and take a more straightforward path.

Social Listening

When buying a product, people place their trust in you and want to receive their money's value. If they are not satisfied with your products or services, it is their right to complain and ask for refunds. You need to listen to your customers' queries and complaints and address them to build an authentic and trustworthy brand. However, stay away from customers who are simply taking advantage of potentially free products or illegitimate refunds.

Try to respond to customers personally by replying to their tweets or sending a private message. Leave your email address or contact details to take it further from there.

Twitter Chats

Using Twitter chats is the ultimate way to grow more connections and followers by delving into the right kind of chat topics with like-minded people and brands. It demands you to be active with conversations, following people and keeping the relations alive after exiting the chat. This is a great way to attract not only random followers but also those who will value your brand and promote it sincerely. You can also start your own chat if you have difficulty in finding one that will help you "fit in". Either way, it surely is great for getting more attention, which will really help your brand. Stay up to date with the topics, and participate in Twitter chats as much as you can. You can also promote your Twitter chats across your other social media platforms to drive your followers to Twitter or use TweetDeck, Twubs, or other similar tools for this purpose.

Strategy 2: Proper Hashtag Use

Everyone knows the importance of hashtags on Twitter. The majority of exploration and searching takes place due to the use of the right hashtags. However, beware; it can cause the complete opposite effect if misused. Depending on the type of brand or content, research the right hashtags or use tools that determine a certain set of hashtags to post with your content. This helps in marking your presence by grouping your content with relevant posts. This way, users can also search your profile easily.

There is also a rising trend of inventing your own hashtag and encouraging your followers to use it to increase interaction. For example, you can organize contests that enable your followers to tag other users with your invented hashtag, which has the potential of going viral and helping you get recognition.

Strategy 3: The Use of Visuals

Visual content has been proven to engage audiences three times more than simple text. Posting visual content shows thoughtfulness and adds personality to your account. Whether it is an image, video, or GIF, followers react more to visual content as it tends to deliver a clearer message and show effort.

Short Videos

Short videos are the truest form of engagement on any social media platform, and this obviously applies to Twitter as well. With the extensive use of smartphones, more people are turning to the mobile application of this platform and driving more than 90 percent of video views. You can either post an already-recorded video or experiment with different video lengths by filming a video directly from your smartphone. And because it plays automatically, your audience is instantly invested in this type of content as they scroll.

GIFs

GIFs are an underrated type of content that can make for powerful marketing action. They are much, much more than short, funny graphics, and can be used to convey robust information that will grab your audience's attention within a short period. You can also edit your visual content and compile cuts to highlight your products or other important information regarding your brand.

Images and Videos

To create visual content in the form of images and videos, you can use the following content ideas to create more engagement:

- Create a video series that rotates around "a typical day in the office" or behind the scenes.
- Interview all employees one by one and make it a weekly type of content.
- Hand over your account to an influencer to fetch more followers and give it a fresh twist.
- Include DIY projects or post "how-to" videos showing your products.
- Conduct quizzes and giveaway contests for more user interaction.
- Go for a crossover with other brands or companies, depending on the type and size of your brand.

• Put live video tweets to use, as mentioned above.

A Few More Tips

While these strategies are important to keep your marketing alive, there are certain things that you still need to pay attention to.

• *Building a Great Profile*

Now that your Twitter account is up and running, it is time to build your profile to create an impact on your followers and future audiences. Apart from writing a brilliant bio that captures the attention of potential followers, you also need to add specific keywords, your location, and certain hashtags that will strengthen your profile. You know you have succeeded in building a top-notch profile when your followers send you direct messages or congratulate you for your real-time presence. Also, you'll probably be gaining followers quickly.

Since this platform allows you to use fewer characters within your bio, you need to be smart in writing a catchy intro as it'll act as a first impression on your followers.

Make your brand seen by further tweaking your profile, using your location and SEO strategies. Also, try to get verified as soon as you can. Getting verified shows your users that you are authentic, and thus, they can trust your brand.

• *Delving into Analytics*

You can use Twitter analytics to measure and reveal statistics behind your account's engagement and followers. You can visualize the demographics of your content, followers, and location. You can also measure the interaction of your followers on every post, such as likes, comments, and retweets. This can give you a clearer picture of the type of content that generates more interaction, thus guiding you in the right direction.

• *Scheduling and Posting*

People are more active on social media, particularly on Twitter, during specific hours of the day. It is the peak time for engagement and the right time to post your content for maximum likes, comments, and retweets before your tweet gets lost in the world of oblivion. The most advisable times to tweet are 12 p.m., 5 p.m., and 6 p.m., but this can vary depending on the type of your followers and content.

How much you post per day matters, too. You need to tweet at least once a day to garner more attention. The more frequently you tweet, the more presence you gain. Try experimenting with different timings and varied frequency to achieve maximum engagement. Schedule your tweets and content accordingly, or use tools to predict the optimum time for posting, and automatically upload content.

Finally, remember to follow your marketing plan. Do not just schedule it and forget about it; be consistent and keep going. It is a slow start for everyone, but eventually, you will build a gigantic community as long as you stay consistent and original.

Chapter 10: Instagram Marketing

Instagram is one of the most popular social media platforms, with a total of more than 800 million users. What is striking about Instagram is that at least 500 million users are active daily, and the growth rate is staggering to the extent that there is an increase of 100 million users per month. This makes it an essential platform for any business to not only appear on but also spread awareness about their brand, driving traffic to their website and boosting their overall sales.

While Instagram users were initially known to be mostly composed of young people, making it extremely beneficial for businesses that target youth, the older generations are also embracing the platform and have started to make an appearance there, which makes it easier for you to reach various types of audiences.

Using Instagram is valuable to your business as the engagement rate on posts—a whopping 4.21 percent—is 58 times higher than Facebook and 120 times higher than Twitter. So, if you are looking to grow your business, reach a wider audience, and get the most ROI, here are three strategies you should be using on Instagram:

Strategy 1: Instagram Stories

One of the things that makes Instagram successful is that its team is always developing the platform and looking for ways to ensure that users will not only continue to use it but also stay longer. One of the features that they added was Instagram stories, and it has become an even more advantageous and useful tool for you to use. That is because 400 million users are scrolling through Instagram stories daily, making story ads an excellent way to reach a larger audience. So, how do you use Instagram stories to your advantage?

Story ads allow your business ad to show up between stories and reach users as they flick through other stories. But what is truly captivating about Instagram stories is that they give you the chance to be so much more fun and creative, as well as visually appealing. Story ads let your business use all the available Instagram story features to put together an ad that's captivating and interesting, or one that requires a user to become more interactive. Here are a few tips to help your business make the most of Instagram stories, especially since the click-through rate on stories is much higher than feed ads, making the return on investment even higher:

Create Fun and Interesting Content

You only have 15 seconds to get your message across and reach your audience, so you really need to make the most of it. However, with the tools available on Instagram stories, you can make your stories eye-catching and interesting. These tools include text overlay, which allows you to highlight the message you want to send and make it stand out—loud and clear. You can also use the GIFs that are installed in the story features, which are definitely funny and cute, and they have the power to captivate the audience with their playfulness.

Use Polls and Sliders

Another feature on Instagram stories that really helps build a relationship with the audience is the use of polls and sliders to get the audience to engage with your business profile. With polls, you can post an image and have users vote for the one they prefer by giving them the option of choosing left or right. You can also ask a question and have them respond by giving them options to vote or using an open-ended reply. However, in most cases, voting gets a higher response as it requires much less effort on the user's part. With sliders, you get the audience to engage just by using a sliding emoji to react to your story and show that they liked it. The reason these Instagram story features are a great form of content is that they require the target audience to engage with your post, which helps you build a warmer relationship with potential customers.

Build a Relationship with Your Audience

Because there are so many businesses out there, most users tend to appreciate getting up close and personal and seeing what happens behind the curtains. You can use Instagram stories to your advantage by allowing your audience to view the behind-the-scenes content. This could be done by showing the process of how your products come to life, taking their opinions on future designs, or even having them see the faces behind the brand and build a personal connection with it through witnessing day-to-day activities. This way, they get to know you and your employees on a personal level. Instagram stories allow you to be funny, unconventional, or personal, as the stories only last for 24 hours, which means you don't need to stick 100 percent to your polished and professional business persona.

Use Consumer-Generated Content

Instagram stories allow your business to get much more interactive with the audience, as many campaigns can be solely led on Instagram. This can be done by asking your audience to post a photo with your product in order to win a free product, show how they used it in a smart, funny, or silly way, or come up with an idea that encourages the user to post on your behalf, tagging your account and helping you reach their audience, too.

Other Tips

Apart from polls, sliders, and user-generated content, there are other ways to get your audience to engage with your stories. Here are a few tips for using this feature effectively:

- **Mentions**

Mentioning another account, user, or even an influencer in your stories is an easy way of getting them to re-post your content on their own stories. This means you get to reach a wider audience.

- Highlights

One of the updated features of Instagram allows you to save stories to your profile as highlights and displays them to other users when they first land on your page. This makes it easier to show them whatever it is that is important to you.

- Geotags

One of the Instagram story features that helps reach a specific audience is the use of geotags. They appeal to users of that specific area as they can connect more with your brand, and they can be viewed by people within that location even if they are not following you.

- Hashtags

Instagram is all about hashtags. Using one in your stories will automatically add it to the list of posts in that hashtag, helping your business become visible to new users and potential followers.

Strategy 2: Shopping Posts

For businesses that use Instagram as a tool to market their products, Instagram Shopping can really help boost sales. Instead of depending on your users having to head to your website, store, or even DM to ask for more information, Instagram Shopping allows them to make a purchase right then and there.

Why is Instagram Shopping a Great Marketing Tool?

- Acts as a Virtual Store for Your Business

With Instagram Shopping, you can now display the prices of your products whenever a user taps on the photo on your feed. To make it even easier for the users to make an instant purchase, they can tap on the price, select the size and color they want, and check out. This also increases the level of engagement on each post; the more people see them, the more taps you get.

- **Allows You to Redirect Traffic to Your Store**

If you do not want to use Instagram as your virtual store and are more interested in gaining more traffic on your website, you could easily redirect users to your store once they have clicked on the post on your feed, checked the price, and decided to make a purchase. Instagram Shopping allows you to add a link to your website or virtual store, and have people perform the transaction there, increasing the traffic on your web page through your Instagram account.

- **Gives Your Business Numerous Ways of Presenting Your Products**

You can choose to display your products in carousel shopping, allowing your business to present a variety of products at the same time due to the ability to tag 20 different products in the same post. This is a great advertising tool, as you can showcase an entire collection and reach more than one audience at a time, while still paying the bare minimum.

Another option is to use a feed post, where you can tag up to five products. This makes it possible for you to put together an entire outfit or display with products that complement each other. You can even post Instagram stories with the tagged products, giving you the ability to use them as story ads.

Setting up Instagram Shopping

If you already have an Instagram account for your business, it is pretty easy to set up Instagram Shopping:

- **Step 1: Make Sure Your Business Account Complies with Instagram Shopping Requirements**

Your business must be located in one of the 46 approved countries, such as the United States, Canada, Puerto Rico, France, United Kingdom, Germany, Italy, Spain, Netherlands, Sweden, Switzerland, Ireland, South Africa, Belgium, Austria, Poland, Greece, Portugal, and more.

Aside from that, you must have a business profile on Instagram and fulfill the requirements for Instagram's merchant agreement and commerce policy.

- **Step 2: Connect Your Instagram Account to a Facebook Catalog**

To set up a catalog of products on Instagram, you must have a Facebook page linked to your Instagram account, with a Facebook catalog displaying your products.

You can do this by going to your Facebook business page and adding a shop section. All you have to do is click on the Shop tab and follow these steps:

1. Press on Set up Shop and agree to the terms and conditions.

2. Enter the business address and click on Next.

3. Choose what currency you would like to use for your Facebook shop, then enter your business email address and click Next.

4. Add your tax registration info.

5. Once you have clicked Finish, you can begin adding products to your shop.

- **Step 3: Your Account will be Verified**

Instagram will then verify your account and check whether you comply with all the requirements before granting you access. It could take quite a while, so be patient.

- **Step 4: Add Product Tags to Your Posts**

Once Instagram has given you the green light and granted you access to Shopping, you can start tagging products on your posts just like you would tag people.

After choosing a photo from your gallery, editing the filters, and adding the captions and hashtags you want to include in your post, you will find a Tag Products option right beneath Tag People. Click on it and start typing the name of the product. Remember: You can tag up to five products in your post. Once you are done, you can share your post, and it will be added to your feed.

Strategy 3: Instagram Ads

With Instagram being so popular, it is a great tool for businesses to use for advertising purposes. It allows you to get much more creative and reach a wider audience, as well as ensuring a greater return on investment due to the high engagement rate, making it an extremely useful and cheap advertising tool. You can even include Instagram ads in your Facebook ad campaigns—it is easy and hassle-free. Here are a few ways through which you can get the optimum results when advertising on Instagram:

Video Ads

Video ads are the future of social media, and that is why it is essential to incorporate them into your advertising strategy. With 72 percent of posts shared on Instagram being photos, videos give your business a real advantage to stand out. However, when using them as an advertising tool, you need to ensure that your videos still have the visual appeal that fits the platform's identity. This can be done by introducing the video with colors and beautiful imagery—also, try to avoid being extremely promotional. To get the best results while using video ads, you should make the video short and captivating by keeping it fun or interesting. You can invoke a certain emotion, offer a quick tip, or a piece of advice.

Another tip when creating video ads is to use vertical videos, as they take up more of the screen space and allow your video to play automatically when someone is scrolling through their feed. This means the ideal video size for Instagram is 600x750 pixels. To grab the user's attention instantly, you need to get right to business and start your video with something appealing to stop the user from scrolling. Even though it is a promotional video, you need to avoid starting your video with a company logo or anything that looks too promotional, or else you will lose their attention right away. Remember that most people have their sound off, to begin with, so you need to use strong visuals to get them to put the sound back on.

GIFs or Boomerangs

Video content does not have to be produced and filmed—it can even be done by using animated GIFs of your products, or even one of your products prettified with an animated GIF tool that will add a bit of authenticity and character to it. Another great option is using Boomerang, which displays a playful movement on the screen, making your product appear so much more appealing. You can use the visuals of a customer using your product, unboxing it, or adding it to a relative environment. It is catchy, short, and will definitely stand out from a sea of photographs, making it a great way to reach your audience and use advertising on Instagram to your advantage.

Influencers

Whether you like the idea of influencers or not, they really help you reach a wider audience and raise awareness about your brand or products. There are so many different levels of influencers on Instagram, and not all of them come with an expensive rate card. You will find mid-range influencers who still have thousands of followers, but not hundreds of thousands or millions, making them a cheaper option.

The reason why collaborating with an influencer yields great results on Instagram is that they have a large fan base of people who look up to them, enjoy their content, and trust them enough to hear what they are saying. Due to the high level of engagement most influencers have, when they give your business a shout-out or mention it in their stories, posts, or short videos, you will most likely gain quite a few followers and let them know that your business exists. However, it is essential to pick the influencer you'll collaborate with carefully, as you want to make sure that the right audience will be targeted and that their image will not harm your business in any way.

Lead Ads

One of the advantages of using lead ads on Instagram is that they do not require the audience to exert much effort, but still allow you to build the first step of a customer relationship without being too promotional. This can be done by asking them to subscribe to your newsletter or receive a tip, freebie, or update via email. However, because Instagram already has all the necessary info stored, it doesn't require the users to fill in their details but displays the automated personal info a customer needs, only requiring them to click "submit".

Story Ads

As mentioned above, Instagram stories are gaining popularity, making them an excellent tool for advertising. While you can choose from many different types of story ads to display to your users, in general, an engaging story will probably perform better. This can be done through polls, sliders, lead ads, or getting users to swipe up and land on your web page. Just keep in mind that you only have 15 seconds to grab their attention, so your ad really needs to be captivating.

There are so many reasons a business needs to have a strong presence on Instagram. As it is a continuously growing platform, it makes for a great marketing tool for any business to use. Helping you reach your marketing goals, whether it is reaching a broader audience, boosting sales, or having a stronger online presence, Instagram is a tool that your business should be using.

Chapter 11: Snapchat Marketing

More than just an entertaining social media platform, Snapchat is extensively used for marketing these days. "But it's nothing more than filters and quirky lenses," you say? Well, brands are now starting to realize the potential of this underrated tool that has evolved over the years. The concept of disappearing images and videos was once considered as weak content that could not garner much interaction. Back then, creating a budget and investing in this platform seemed like a waste of time and money. However, with a lot of experiments and some notable experience spanning many years, this concept has turned out to be a powerful strategy for all brands who are trying to make their mark online.

Snapchat once witnessed a low point after its launch, but then escalated rapidly between the years 2015 and 2016, when users doubled from 100 million to 200 million worldwide. Around 75 percent of these users are active daily on Snapchat, spending around 25 to 30 minutes on the app every day. If your brand is targeting a younger audience, such as users in their early 20s and the Gen Z population, Snapchat is the right platform for you.

Why Snapchat?

A few astonishing stats revealed the power of this social media platform and how it could be a major tool for your business in driving more revenue and sales. As mentioned, Snapchat caters to over 200 million users who collectively watch more than 10 billion videos daily. While users watch this bewildering number of videos, they enthusiastically contribute to it and produce over 3 billion videos daily, 76 percent of which include online shopping products. Snapchat has recently overtaken other platforms like Twitter, LinkedIn, and Pinterest, with more registered users who are active regularly. A significant chunk of such users is based in the United States and North America.

Reasons to Include Snapchat in Your Marketing Plan

• Provides a Different Kind of Engagement

This book has discussed over and over again how stories, as a concept for engagement, have boomed. And that is what Snapchat is all about; images and videos that disappear after 24 hours. Users are bound to remember moving images and videos better than stationary text content. Stories provide you with the opportunity to form creative content that stays fresh and does not become repetitive. Your users will most likely not recall content that was posted a few months ago, which can be a major advantage. You can create campaigns or snippets of your long videos to offer your users a sneak peek of your next project, like Taco Bell has been doing for a while.

• Ranks Among the Least Competitive Platforms

As mentioned at the beginning of this chapter, Snapchat has been underestimated as a marketing platform. Many brands are still avoiding its use and turning to Instagram, Facebook, and Twitter. It is high time that you tapped into this platform and made the most of it. Since a lot of brands and companies have yet to discover the potential of Snapchat for marketing, there is less competition there. It's the right time to establish your presence and create engagement through this platform.

• Laid-Back

If your company or business demands a rather professional and formal language for user engagement, Snapchat is not for you. However, this platform has given a certain personality to most of the brands that use it. With disappearing content, filters, lenses, doodles, real-time videos, and bitmojis, this medium is fresh, raw, and quirky, hence attracting a younger crowd. It doesn't pressure you or your brand into being more formal. In fact, it encourages you to be more open and interactive with your followers, showing them your brand's real face.

- **Tech-Driven**

Many social media platforms today use technologically updated features such as geolocations and augmented reality. Snapchat started it all. With new filters, lenses, and features that are updated every once in a while, within the app, Snapchat can be called a tech-savvy platform. This book has discussed the onset, importance, and future of augmented reality in the previous chapters, along with how users and potential followers can be lured in with this feature for effective marketing.

Strategy 1: Linked Stories

The "swipe up" feature in Snapchat has been handy since its introduction, especially for brands and companies who are trying to generate revenue through social media. You can now attach links of websites or apps to any story or snap that you send to your customers, and it has become one of the most powerful marketing strategies. Once your customers click on the "swipe up" link, they are directed to a new window that will either contain a relevant article or your website. Functioning rather as ads, the concept of linked stories will be discussed further in this chapter. But before that, first, understand the procedure of attaching links to your stories.

➢ Click on a relevant image or record a video based on your content requirement, or upload a picture from your gallery. Add filters, emojis, music, and stickers if you prefer.

➢ When you check the snap preview, you'll see an icon that represents linking websites and URLs.

➤ You'll get a Type a URL option. Copy and paste the URL of the website you want to link, or type it in if you remember. You can view this link in a window within the app.

➤ Next, you can find an Attach to Snap option at the bottom of the page. Tap it to link the website with your image or video. You can now send it to your friends or put it up as a story.

This helpful feature can also be used within chats. You just need to copy and paste the URLs in the chats or directly type them while replying to your friends. Even though this feature has been up and running since July 2017, not many companies are taking advantage of it. So, it is a good idea to link your stories directly with your company's shopping page or blog by creating compelling content to drive more sales and increase traffic.

Strategy 2: Behind-the-Scenes Snaps

This is, by far, the rawest form of engagement any brand can offer. By showing behind-the-scenes content to your followers, you increase your chances for interaction and engagement as they tend to trust you more. These exclusive peeks and insights into your office and employees will be highly appreciated by your audience. It is truly a delight to watch the making of people's favorite products, and the work put in by every member of your team. When your customers know and have access to everything that goes on in the backstage of your work, they can fully trust you by becoming familiar with your company's vibe and character.

How to Use Behind-the-Scenes Content on Snapchat

• A Day in your Office

Shoot an entire day at your workplace and highlight all the peak points in a regular workday that make it exciting. Begin by entering your office, having standard interactions and conversations with your colleagues as you normally would, and add a few glimpses of important moments.

- **Employee Q&A**

Let your entire team handle your brand's Snapchat account and conduct interviews among themselves—or any enthusiastic followers once you get a few. Include answers to questions like "Why do you like working here?" and "How has this brand become an integral part of your life?"

- **How it's Made**

If you have a factory or a workshop that manufactures your products, take your followers on a virtual tour to show them how your products are made. This will showcase the true quality of your products and prove to your customers that you are not afraid to show them the process.

- **Humor and Fun**

If your team consists of hilarious people, you can conduct a few pranks or riddle quizzes among them, or simply create funny content to keep your audience thoroughly engaged. Funny content is bound to spread and be shared more often, keeping your customers and followers waiting for more.

Strategy 3: Snapchat Ads

Snapchat Ads is a new feature designed for marketers and content creators, and it is a raging success. This new update has allowed brands and companies to reach millions of users worldwide and create brand awareness. Whether you need to drive sales or increase traffic on your website and social media platforms, Snapchat Ads cater to all purposes. This feature allows users to visit your website directly or drive local followers and users to your store. It also leads them to download your app by creating a path toward the Play Store or App Store.

You can sandwich your ads between your stories after carefully planning a day's content or any campaign. By showing your followers your intent and purpose, you can get them interested in swiping up the link on the ad. As mentioned, you can direct them to your website, online store, app, AR lens, or video to increase interaction and engagement.

Types of Ads

Snapchat offers a lot of advertisement options that are super effective in increasing followers and engagement. Depending on your brand and the content you create, the following features or ad types can be used to promote your products or services flawlessly.

- **Collection Ads**

Mainly useful for shopping and driving sales, Collection Ads allow you to show a range of products that can be viewed with simple taps and bought easily through a swipe-up link to your website or online store.

- **Snap Ads**

Consisting of a single image or video, Snap Ads provides you with the layout of an image, video, or GIF that lets users access your brand's website or app's link with just a single swipe.

- **Story Ads**

This feature displays your ad in the form of a "Discover" tile with other popular and trending ads and stories on your users' feeds. This targets your potential users based on the relevant demographics.

- **Filters and Lenses**

You can now create your own filters and lenses, and customize them to your brand's image. It is an impeccable way to generate interaction with your users through augmented reality and playful filters.

- **Non-Skippable Videos or Commercials**

Similar to Instagram and Facebook, you can also create non-skippable, commercial-quality video content to serve as ads for your brand. You can place them among your premium, widespread content,

Snapchat Ads Manager

With the business version of Snapchat, you can create ads on the go. This social media platform has created Ads Manager, which is a self-serve tool to create ads. It gives you the flexibility to create an amazing image and video content and manage your ads at absolutely no cost. Once you have your account set up on Ads Manager, you are good to go. Not only can you create content and plan your campaigns through this free tool, but you can also choose your audience depending on your location, and analyze the performance of your ads.

In the Ads Manager window, you can access the Dashboard and Creative Library keys to create, edit, and view your ads. The Custom Audiences option allows you to choose and target your audience depending on your brand, location, and other demographics. Lastly, the Help Center helps you navigate your way through Ads Manager and guides you through common issues.

Take a look at the way Ads Manager works and some necessary steps to take:

1. First, identify the main objective behind your ad or campaign—whether it is to generate more leads, increase followers, or just spread brand awareness.

2. Set a start and end date with a proper schedule for your ad, in addition to choosing a name.

3. Depending on the age, gender, location, language, demographics, and type of followers, define your target audience using the available options.

4. Next, set a budget, the minimum being $100. This allows Snapchat to show your ads to users who are interested in your business and likely to buy your products or install your app.

5. Choose your snap-type from the options Top Snap Only, Web View, App Install, and Long Form Video. Create your headline, write your brand name, and finally, select your call-to-action option.

After you have launched your ad, you can monitor its performance through the ad metrics feature. It notifies you of your campaign's reach, the money spent, and the impressions it has made. It is highly recommended that you use Ads Manager if you are planning on using Snapchat as your marketing platform.

Additional Tips

These three strategies can become major guiding principles for your Snapchat marketing plan. However, to make it even better, you need to follow these important tips:

Don't Cross-Post

While people know that Instagram and Facebook copied Snapchat's original concept of posting content through stories, it still holds its authentic authority. However, a few brands cross-post the same content on Snapchat, Instagram, Facebook, and Twitter, over and over again. At some point, it gets monotonous and boring. If you do this, you could end up losing many followers on all your social media platforms, which could be risky for your brand, especially if you are running a business online.

Plan your content differently for all the social media platforms you are using, and try not to be repetitive. You might run out of ideas sometimes, and cross-posting once in a while is still okay. But doing it regularly is a big no-no. Keep your content diverse but follow your brand's language. It will make your followers curious and urge them to follow your brand on every social media platform to know what is cooking.

Reach the Right Audience

At times, even if you sell products that are efficient and show a lot of potentials, you can fail to drive sales and generate the targeted revenue over a specific period. You might also be on the right track when it comes to social media marketing. So, what could be wrong? A major factor that could disrupt your interaction with followers—and lead to poor sales—might be your business's inability to reach the relevant audience. You need to reach the accessible Snapchatters that would genuinely be interested in your products.

You can target users based on their age, household income, gender, likes and dislikes, habits, country, and city. Snapchat offers you some amazing tools to identify and target your potential customers, which could completely change your social media marketing game and generate more sales.

Like other social media platforms, Snapchat can also be intimidating at first. You just need to remain patient and be consistent to establish your brand's presence and create spectacular engagement. Now that you have read about various social media platforms in detail, it is time to build on this information and formulate your marketing plan. However, before you get to that, keep reading to learn more about influencer marketing and the top tools you can use this year to polish your marketing strategies, as well as the future of social media marketing to help you stay ahead of the game.

Chapter 12: The Rise of Influencer Marketing and How to Use It

Influencer marketing is a great marketing tool for your business due to its extreme effectiveness. Not only have 86 percent of marketers been actively using influencer marketing, but also the number of Google searches for "influencer marketing" has increased by 1,500 percent over the past three years.

The reason why influencer marketing has become imperative for businesses to include in their marketing strategies is that influencers on social media help you reach your specific target audience and increase their awareness of your brand. That is because social media influencers have a large following, as well as a strong connection and relationship with their fan base. This makes your target audience reliable, loyal, and willing to accept and follow the advice of their role models.

Why Is Influencer Marketing on the Rise?

Celebrity marketing has been used for decades, where a celebrity would endorse a certain brand, becoming the brand's image or being seen using its products. However, using a celebrity is not only a costly method of advertising but also not quite as effective—since most people are aware of the fact that it is a marketing strategy.

Nowadays, with social media giving regular customers a voice, it has enabled people who are interested in a specific sector to get more recognition because of their authenticity and awareness. As people with the same interests start to follow their journeys, the number of their followers increase, turning them into an influencer. Because they are real-life customers who offer authentic and valuable information and reviews to their followers, they are considered role models who have the power to affect the choices their followers make. Based on statistics provided by Mediakix, 80 percent of marketers agree that influencer marketing is effective, and 71 percent also conclude that the customers generated by influencer marketing are of excellent quality.

As a marketer, using influencers to help promote a business is an excellent way to reach an audience that is not only interested in what your business offers, but will also become potential buyers, leading to a boost in sales and revenue. That is because the fan base of influencers usually consists of those who share an interest in the niche market that you are part of, and they tend to follow these influencers to gain more knowledge about that sector. The difference between influencers and celebrities is that the level of trust, loyalty, and engagement on an influencer's social media platforms is so much higher, making the ROI and outcome of influencer marketing much more beneficial for your business.

How Does a Business Use Influencer Marketing?

There are numerous influencers available for every sector you can think of. You will find travel, fashion, food, lifestyle, and beauty influencers; vloggers and bloggers; advocates for human rights, LGBTQ+ rights, and gender equality; as well as people who fight for any other social or environmental cause, and many others.

So, the first thing businesses should do is figure out who the influencers in their sectors are. This can be done by checking your followers, as you might find that some of your customers are influencers who believe in your brand and what you have to offer. You can also analyze the other people your fans follow and pinpoint whom they find to be influential.

Once you have identified the best influencers to use, then you have two options: try to reach out to them on their social media platforms, or contact an agency and have them give you access to the influencers.

What Can an Influencer Do for Your Business?

The advantage of working with niche influencers is that it generates the exact type of target audience you are looking for—the people who are most likely to become potential customers. All you have to do is choose the type of influencer who is in line with your brand and relevant to your niche market.

In fact, many businesses tend to use influencer marketing to raise awareness about their brands. Statistics show that 37 percent of marketers have admitted to using influencer marketing to build brand awareness because of how effective it is, but that is not the only reason. Here are several other ways your business can benefit from working with influencers:

Review Your Products or Services

One of the most common ways of using an influencer is by sending them a product to use or having them try out your services firsthand. Afterward, they give their honest opinion and offer reviews about their experience with your brand. This helps your business gain more potential customers, as working with a niche influencer gives you access to the right target audience.

Give your Business a Shout-Out

Whether it is through a post, short video, or even stories, an influencer giving your business a shout-out will help their fan base get familiar with what your brand has to offer. This can be a great way to generate more targeted followers.

Take Over Your Account

Another way of using an influencer for marketing purposes is by carrying out a social media take-over. The influencer will have access to your account and interact with your audience directly. This way, your followers can ask questions, and the influencer will answer them, offering them insight into their day and giving them a chance to connect with a person they look up to. Because influencers tend to announce on their social media platforms that they will be taking over your account, you'll find their followers also heading to your account, bringing you more traffic and engagement, and spreading awareness about your products or services.

Collaboration

You can choose to collaborate with an influencer by having them announce your latest campaigns, give their followers a discount code for your products, or even become a brand ambassador for your business. All these can really help boost sales, as their fan base will have a lot of faith and trust in the influencer's recommendations.

Create Content

Many people tend to use influencers because they are great at creating authentic and real video content that appeals to the consumer. Instead of spending large sums of money on professional video production, you can spend a fraction of that price on hiring an influencer who will create engaging content for your brand. That way, you will ensure that the engagement level will be extremely high, as they have their family, friends, and followers to vouch for them.

Micro-Influencers vs. Celebrity Influencers: Which Type of Influencer Is Best for Your Business?

When it comes to influencers, there is always the dilemma of which type to use. There are celebrity influencers who have hundreds of thousands of followers and sometimes even millions, whereas micro-influencers have thousands or tens of thousands of followers. So, how do you choose which one is better for your business?

The number of followers is not always the most important factor you should be analyzing; instead, you should be looking at the engagement rate to help you decide. In most cases, you will find that the more followers an influencer gets, the less engagement they have, indicating that more followers don't always mean more interaction.

On the contrary, since niche fans are aware of the identity of their influencers and choose whom they want to support and look up to, they tend to have more faith and loyalty in smaller-sized influencers. They feel they can relate to them and trust their judgment. Most people know that the bigger the fan base, the more an influencer is approached by brands, making them lose their credibility and authenticity in the long run.

Benefitting from Micro-Influencers

Here are a few reasons why instead of opting for a few celebrity influencers, you should use ten to 20 micro-influencers:

- **Higher Engagement Rates**

HelloSociety has found that micro-influencers or accounts with 30,000 or fewer followers are much more beneficial to marketers. That is because these influencers tend to deliver 60 percent higher engagement rates as their fan base is smaller, more engaged, and more loyal.

- **Cost-Effective**

One of the advantages of using influencer marketing is that it is incredibly cost-effective. In fact, influencers are 6.7 times more cost-effective than celebrities, and they create 22 times as much buzz. This means that every dime you are paying is worth it, and the return on investment is really high.

- **Cheaper**

Because micro-influencers are much cheaper, they allow your business to use several influencers at the same cost as using one or two celebrity influencers. This gives you the advantage of reaching a wider, more precise audience that will really help grow your business more effectively.

- **Diverse Content**

Using several micro-influencers allows you to get creative with your business and try out different strategies to see which resonates best with the audience. That not only makes your brand look creative and innovative but also offers the user a variety of content to choose from, as well as catering to different audiences. For example, you can ask one influencer to post on their social media platforms, another one to get their audience to take part in a campaign, a third one to create video content, and a fourth one to review or test out your products. This will allow you to have interesting and engaging content, in addition to making your brand look like it is super exposed and popular among most of the influencers in that niche.

- **Easier to Reach and Communicate With**

Most micro-influencers will respond to your inquiries via social media, instead of you having to hire an agency to get through to them. They are also less picky and more open to several suggestions, making them much easier to deal with.

- **Higher ROI**

As mentioned above, because of the power influencers have over their audience, they can direct them to your business and products, convincing them to test them out. This means that every dime you spend on influencer marketing comes with a higher ROI, making it a great marketing tactic to use.

If you are wondering whether your business should be working with influencers, then the answer is definitely "Yes!" Not only is the rise in influencer marketing growing, but it is also extremely effective, powerful, and helpful when it comes to reaching the precise audience you need for your business to grow. However, you need to choose the influencers carefully by analyzing their content, followers, and personalities to make sure that they are relevant to your brand and comply with its identity. Working with influencers will also help you produce creative content that will appeal to your consumers and really tap into different audiences, which will grow your social media presence, boost your sales, increase your followers, and provide you with loyal customers who believe in your brand and what you have to offer.

Chapter 13: Top 7 Social Media Tools for 2020

Growing your social media organically is not an easy task, but it is not impossible either. With the right tools and a good understanding of the different data you can make use of, you can really optimize your content to be more visible, sought-after, and useful for your target audience. In order for you to do this, here are some useful tools for organic growth that you can explore in 2020:

1. TubeBuddy

Because video content is a key focus in 2020, you should be ensuring that you are stepping up your game on YouTube and focusing on video content that is useful, highly searchable, and appealing to a wide audience. That is where TubeBuddy comes in; it gives your business a competitive edge when you're trying to figure out what type of content to create and optimizing your video to make sure that it ranks highly on the search tabs. If you're new to TubeBuddy, you'll find that there's a free version and paid version. Once you've downloaded TubeBuddy, you can choose which one works best for you by skimming through the available features, but it is always a good idea to test the free version first and make sure you're comfortable with it before you go all in. For the most part, the free version still allows you to make use of many important features, such as the following:

Worthy Content Creation

One of the main advantages of using TubeBuddy is that it helps you find content that is searchable and optimizes your keywords for SEO purposes. Say that you are in the fitness industry and are wondering what type of content you should be putting out there. Naturally, the first thing that would come to mind is something about weight loss. To check whether this is a topic worth pursuing, you can add it to the search bar on TubeBuddy, and you will be presented with a keyword score that gives you the answer. This depends on the search volume, determining whether it is a topic that's widely searched, as well as the amount of competition available in terms of the existing content on that topic.

When the topic is highly searched and included in a lot of content that has already been created, it will be difficult for your video to rank high and get the recognition it deserves—in that case, that topic is not worth pursuing. However, TubeBuddy also provides you with related searches to give you other topic ideas. For example, one of the ideas that show up in related searches is "How to lose weight fast without exercise". When checking the keyword score, it changes from poor to good because it is highly searched, but there is not as much content available on this specific topic, making it an option you could consider. This helps you understand that the content you will create will rank high and be visible to your audience, too. You don't just want to create content that is highly searched; you also want it to be visible on the first page of search results so that people can find it easily. That's how you decide whether it's worth it or not.

Keyword Research

TubeBuddy also allows you to find out what keywords a competitor's video includes through tags. This way, you can get a better understanding of your own keywords and how to optimize them to make your video more visible and searchable.

If you look at a successful video with over one million views, TubeBuddy does not just show you the keywords but also how the video ranks for each keyword. The reason why it's helpful is that it will inspire you to target better keywords by looking at what your competitors are using. You will see what's working for them and ensure that you are optimizing your keywords to make them more visible and rank higher on YouTube.

2. Keywords Everywhere

Keywords Everywhere is a Google plug-in extension that is a great tool for SEO optimization. It helps you with keyword research and is beneficial when it comes to content creation. It gives you content ideas based on the most popular searches.

Say that you work in sustainable fashion and want to create content around that topic. If you were to insert that keyword, Keyword Everywhere would give you insight into how many times a month this keyword has been searched, to help you decide whether it is worth creating content with it. This tool also gives you related keywords and other content that people who searched for sustainable fashion could be interested in, based on their searches. Having this insight really helps you understand the user, their interests, and what would make for beneficial content to use. By using it, you can create data-driven content that is searchable and ensure that your content is useful and visible to the audience.

3. Flume

If you are looking for a tool to make Instagram much more flexible for your business needs, then Flume is one you should consider. It allows you to reply to DMs straight from your computer to up your DM game on Instagram and stay on track of customer interaction. Through the conversations featured on Flume, you can respond to your DMs and quickly filter them. You can view the unread messages only, and be sure to respond to all those you haven't replied to yet.

You can also search for hashtags to understand how significant they are and decide which ones to include in your posts. By optimizing your posts this way, you will be making them visible to a broader audience. Flume will also make it much easier for you to create a connection with your followers, stay on top of your game, and respond to DMs promptly.

4. Later

Another Instagram tool you should consider using is Later. This tool allows you to plan your feed, schedule your posts, and auto-publish, so you do not have to worry about posting each one separately. You can automatically tag people in your posts, meaning that you don't have to be glued to your phone to use Instagram. It will allow you to pre-plan and schedule your content while using Instagram to your advantage.

Comment Features

The paid version of Later also allows you to reply to comments on your computer, making it easier and faster to connect with your audience. This is important because the latest Instagram algorithm requires you to be active in the comments section. The more comments you receive and write, the more reach your posts get. This, in turn, increases your chances of being visible on other people's feeds and getting a higher rate of engagement on your posts.

The tool also shows you all the comments that you have received on different posts to allow you to respond to them quickly, which will be beneficial in terms of growing faster and building a better relationship with your audience.

Instagram Analytics Tool

With Later's Instagram Analytics tool, you can get an overview of how your account is doing and monitor your analytics through useful graphs. Sure, you can use Instagram's own analytics tool for this purpose as well, but the audience analytics on Later offer more details that can be very helpful to your business. That is because these can aid you in figuring out what the best days and times to post are, leading to more engagement on your posts. This tool can even tell you the specific hour when you have the most followers online, so you can post at that time and maximize your engagement.

Looking at your demographics and seeing the breakdown of your audience will give you a better understanding of how many users you have in each country—instead of just the top five—as well as the main languages they speak. This can help you decide what language to use in your posts when targeting a specific audience.

Hashtag Features

You can follow hashtags on Later to help you repost trending content on specific topics, just by clicking on them and adding them to your library to post later.

If you are looking to schedule your stories and find hashtags, you will also be able to do that on Later. You can click on hashtag suggestions, enter a keyword, and be given a list of popular hashtags that are relevant to this keyword.

5. Your Analytics

One of the key tools you should be using this year is your very own analytics. Each platform has its own analytics tool to help you get a better understanding of how your posts are performing. They also provide you with detailed insight into your audience so that you can optimize your content accordingly. On Instagram, for example, if you head to View Insights and swipe up, you will see even more data that is collected by Instagram. You can learn about how people found your post, and whether they are following you or not, you can get an idea of where they're coming from, and also determine whether your hashtag strategy is on point or not. If many people are not actually following you or found you through your hashtags, it is a great indication that your hashtags are optimized.

Another advantage of using analytics is that it helps you analyze your content and see how each post has performed. You can get an understanding of your reach per post, how many profile visits and likes you got, what your level of engagement is, etc. This helps you understand what kind of content has been more successful and engaging, giving you an idea of what is working for your brand. Getting an overview of other things like the number of saves and website clicks, as well as which posts made people visit your profile or generated website clicks, will also be beneficial to gain perspective on what kind of content works best for your audience.

6. Anchor

While video content is here to stay, many people are also heading toward audio content, as they are not always available to sit down and watch a video. That is why podcasts are becoming extremely popular, and they are one of the channels your business should focus on this year. The anchor is the tool you should be using to figure out how to use podcasts and have an all-in-one solution to get you started, as well as get distribution to iTunes and Spotify. Voice marketing is set to be huge in 2020, and it's a key strategy you can use to reach a wider audience.

7. Quora

If you are a content-based business, then Quora is an essential tool you should capitalize on to help you understand what people are asking questions about in your niche. It also helps you identify yourself and your business as a leader in the field by answering these questions. Not only that, but you can take those answers and turn them into immediate content by posting them on your blog, or creating a video about them. Quora will give you fresh ideas on content creation, as well as ensuring that you're tackling issues that people are curious about.

Using these tools to your business's advantage will be an extremely effective move. They will allow you to make use of important data and create content that is visible and optimized. This way, your content will rank high and reach a broader audience, making your business grow organically, and fast.

Chapter 14: The Future of Social Media Marketing

Social media is constantly changing; just when you think you have got it all figured out, the platforms update their algorithms, and you are back to square one. That is why you must stay up to date, always be on the lookout for new pieces of information you can implement, and be willing to test out new strategies and tactics to ensure that your social media platforms are not outdated. To help you do that, here are some tips you can implement to keep up with the times:

Focus on User Engagement

On any given day, your posts on social media will most likely reach 1 percent of your followers. While that does sound like a tiny number, you can change your perspective and try to capitalize on that 1 percent. If you start keeping an eye on who actually reads your posts and interacts with them regularly, you can build on that and form a strong relationship with them. As a business, you can do this by always replying to their comments, or even reaching out and giving them a discount because they are considered to be loyal customers. Building relationships and engaging with your users on a personal level is the future of social media, and that is what will differentiate you from AI, which will not tailor feedback and responses to suit different people's reactions and characteristics. Using this tactic is an excellent way to turn those clicks and interactions into conversions.

Build Relationships

Another form of user engagement that is essential to the present and the future of social media marketing is creating content that will truly connect the user to your brand rather than focus on being promotional. Nobody goes on social media to be sold stuff, and that is why your content must focus on building relationships rather than selling products. The stronger the bond, the higher the possibility of conversion, but it's important to focus on creating that bond in the first place. If you create content that is useful, emotional, or funny without the intent of selling, a user is more prone to like, comment, or share your posts, allowing your content to reach a wider audience.

However, it is also useful to understand that a post can go viral based on the real comments that are visible on it. It's not just about likes or shares; the greatest strength lies in comments that go back and forth. That is why it's important always to give the users something to respond to in order to keep the conversation flowing. The more comments a post receives, the more likely it is that Facebook or Instagram will show the post to other people. But that's not the only benefit—once again, you will also be building a relationship in the process and making users feel more connected to your brand.

Create Your Own Influencers

While influencer marketing is still on the rise, its success might be temporary. That is why, as a business, you need to be prepared to have your own influencers. This means that you need to look into your own network, figure out who has influence, and use them to your advantage. Your employees, followers, and even your CEO might have some power that you should be using. The more connected to the brand a person is, the more power they will have when it comes to reaching the audience. Instead of looking for people with a high following, start looking for those within your network who are continually on social media, have the skill of building virtual relationships and engaging with their followers, and use them as the face and voice of the company. Users want to feel an individual connection to a business, and that's why personal branding is a huge and successful field that companies need to tap into from a different perspective. Utilizing the voice of those within your company—and who are familiar with your brand—will add a whole lot of authenticity to your business, instead of using the same strategies and tactics that everyone else is using.

Capitalize on Omnichannel Marketing

It is not enough to be on one platform anymore. To increase your rating and traffic, you need to be sharing to different platforms, targeting different audiences, and directing them to your websites. The more traffic you have, the higher the possibility of conversion rates, making it much more beneficial for a business. However, it is not smart to re-share content on different channels, especially when the content does not fit the identity and strategy of a specific platform. For example, if you want to spread an article, sharing it on your Instagram account with a screenshot of the headline will be quite pointless, as the user will not put effort into searching for the title. However, if you share it on your stories with a swipe-up link, it might be useful. You will realize that going for omnichannel marketing will make your cost-per-click go down, as it helps improve your numbers on all platforms.

Concentrate on Content Marketing

While many people have actually stopped reading, having your own content on your blog or website is still extremely advantageous, and is likely to stay that way in the future. That is because the content will redirect users to your products, and it can be used as a tool to generate conversions through search engine optimization. You can use more than one advertising tool to suit different kinds of people through Google ads, Facebook ads, and SEO.

Content will also allow you to tap into different markets that are underused and help you reap many benefits, such as translations. Instead of creating new content, your business can decide to target a different audience by translating the existing content into a language that does not involve as much competition as English. That way, you will make use of the people searching for this information, who will get familiar with what you have to offer just because they do not have enough resources available in their own language. Tapping into a market with a strong audience will enable you to dominate it quickly, maintain stability for a long while, and generate more revenue.

Use User Metrics to Beat Google

There is probably a lot of content that your business put out there without much of an outcome. Instead of throwing it away and deeming it useless, you can try and beat Google by playing by its own rules. In most cases, you will find that the reason why your posts did not perform well was that they weren't optimized with the necessary keywords to be visible on Google. And what does that mean? It means you have the opportunity to transform useless content into winning content just by making a few changes.

All you have to do is look for keywords that have less than a 5 percent click-through rate, and pages that have less than a 4 percent click-through rate and make sure that the keywords that you rank for are in the title tag as well as within the actual content. Once you make those changes, you'll have Google recrawl your site, and your click-through rate will skyrocket. To have the upper hand, you should be using list-related numbers and keywords such as "how-to, free, you, tips, blog post, why, best, tricks, and great". The next step is to wait for a month until Google has the chance to spread your posts to those searching for them, and then you'll see amazing results. Understanding the user and what they are searching for is the key to winning on all platforms.

Remember the Importance of Branding

Branding is not just used to identify your products or services, but it is beneficial to help you grow your brand for marketing purposes. That is because the bigger your brand, the more likely your content is to go viral. To cut down on fake news, most social media platforms determine authenticity based on size. So, when you have a larger number of followers, your content is more likely to be real, making it more visible than that of smaller companies in the same market. That's why focusing on growing your brand and social media presence with engaging content—without the sole intent of selling—will help your numbers grow, as the audience will get more interested in your content. There are also several tools you can use to grow your brand, which seems to be here to stay in the future, such as email marketing, push notifications, or a combination of both.

Don't Restrict Yourself to Conventional Traffic Methods

While pop-ups, quizzes, and newsletters are still useful for a business, they are not enough to help you stay ahead of the game. Look around you, and you will notice that because everyone is using these tactics, they are no longer effective. To stand out and offer something different and more powerful, you need to provide each user with a personalized experience.

The future of social media marketing is all about personalization. Your value as a marketer will lie in your ability to offer a personalized experience, as you'll be able to read different users and adapt to each one separately. While there are many data analysis tools out there, most of them do not factor in human differences—doing this will give you an advantage over the automated systems that are swooping up the market and trying to take your place. One of the most useful tools you'll have at hand is chats. Being able to speak to a customer, build a connection, and adapt to what they need will most likely translate into a conversion. In fact, the chat is now responsible for 28 percent of sales, and that's why the more personalization and authenticity you provide, the higher your conversion rates will be.

Think Like a Winner

Looking at some of the most successful people in the world, you will realize that the reason why they reached their true potential is that they had someone to guide them along the way—also, they never gave up. It is not enough to follow the trends because they are constantly changing. To become successful, you need to think like a winner and always be willing to acquire new information, test out different formulas, and be open to new ideas that could keep you on top. While some of them may not be useful, you just might find yourself setting a new trend and capitalizing on it before anyone else comes on board and reaps the benefits. Besides, you don't have to spend a fortune to gain new knowledge; there is a lot of free information available, just waiting for you to benefit from it.

You need to face the reality that marketing never stops. What works today won't necessarily work tomorrow, and the best approach is always to keep testing and learning in order to be prepared for the future. You will likely be bombarded with a whole lot of information, which will probably overwhelm you, but as long as you try one new thing at a time, you'll always be part of the change.

Conclusion

Thank you for making it to the end of this book. It should have been informative and provided you with all of the tools you need to achieve your goals.

The next step is to implement the important lessons, tips, and advice you learned. Remember that gaining knowledge is the most crucial step in setting up your business. However, it is how you apply what you have learned that will determine whether you will be successful.

Therefore, keep on learning, consult with your peers in the industry, watch for new developments, and always remain observant and positive.

Good luck with promoting your business in the world of social media!

Finally, if you found this book useful in any way, a review on Amazon is always appreciated.

Resources

https://www.contentfac.com/9-reasons-social-media-marketing-should-top-your-to-do-list/

https://www.oberlo.com/blog/social-media-marketing-statisticsht

https://www.smartinsights.com/social-media-marketing/social-media-strategy/new-global-social-media-research/

https://www.business2community.com/social-media/where-social-media-is-headed-in-2020-02266862

https://influencermarketinghub.com/social-media-trends/

https://www.socialmediatoday.com/news/6-key-social-media-trends-to-watch-in-2020/568481/

https://www.entrepreneur.com/article/343863

https://www.business2community.com/social-media/social-media-marketing-how-to-create-a-strong-personal-brand-02250816

https://thenextscoop.com/amazing-tips-help-personal-brand-grow-social-media/

https://blog.hootsuite.com/target-market/

https://promorepublic.com/en/blog/10-ways-find-audience-social-media/

https://devrix.com/tutorial/tips-grow-audience-stand-out-social-media/

https://www.lyfemarketing.com/blog/best-social-media-platforms/

https://buffer.com/library/social-media-sites

https://blog.hootsuite.com/how-to-advertise-on-facebook/

https://www.unboxsocial.com/blog/youtube-marketing-strategy2020/

https://www.youtube.com/watch?v=H3sIHuMMZec

https://www.youtube.com/watch?v=Ysm6CjDuKHs

https://digitalagencynetwork.com/best-twitter-marketing-strategies-to-use-in-2019/

https://blog.hootsuite.com/twitter-marketing/

https://coschedule.com/blog/how-to-use-instagram-stories/

https://later.com/blog/instagram-shopping/

https://www.youtube.com/watch?v=Q_xz4FMlljs

https://moosend.com/blog/snapchat-for-business/

https://www.lsb.com/blog/snapchat-clickable-links/

https://www.entrepreneur.com/article/338115

https://shanebarker.com/blog/rise-of-influencer-marketing/

https://www.youtube.com/watch?v=popowMuKyjY

https://www.youtube.com/watch?v=vqd2pzP5cjw

https://www.youtube.com/watch?v=3frb1JFzEKE

https://www.netbase.com/blog/social-media-tools-2020/

Neil Patel: https://www.youtube.com/watch?v=bGQG_-OG6fs

Carlos Gil: https://www.youtube.com/watch?v=apmIEnJIOm8

Frazer Brookes: https://www.youtube.com/watch?v=LL5b4p3TXL8

Part 2: Instagram Marketing

Unlock the Secrets to Using this Social Media Platform for Personal Branding, Growing Your Small Business and Connecting with Influencers Who Will Grow Your Brand

INSTAGRAM MARKETING

Unlock the Secrets to Using this Social Media Platform for Personal Branding, Growing Your Small Business and Connecting with Influencers Who Will Grow Your Brand

CHASE BARLOW

Introduction

Instagram today is more than a few images of your trip or the delicious breakfast you had this morning, and much more than a couple of likes. It's about producing quality content to catch users' attention; recruiting undiscovered talent; buying and selling products; and a platform to voice your opinions and support causes. More importantly, now is the right time to use this resourceful medium for your business, to get the maximum recognition. In fact, Instagram marketing has been so successful recently that it has beaten the quintessential TV commercials, because the market is digitally active and tech-driven now.

If you're here because you need help in marketing your brand on Instagram, you're in the right place. This book contains all the latest information, significant stats and data, up-to-date advice, and a few personal insights that could turn this entertainment platform into a money-making asset.

Since every person and their dog seems to be on Instagram now, why aren't you? Even though it might seem like an insignificant move at the moment, trust us, it's worth the effort. We've seen brands and businesses blooming on this platform that wouldn't have such a massive fan following or customer base otherwise. It really is the biggest marketing boon in today's digital world. And if you're just a beginner, feeling like a child lost in the woods, this book is here to guide you. From the very basics of signing up on Instagram and setting up your profile, to mastering advanced marketing strategies, these chapters will provide you with valuable insights into gaining followers, turning clicks to leads, and driving sales.

If you're thinking of jumping on the Instagram marketing bandwagon this year, this is a great place to start. With around 1 billion active users on this platform—33% of whom are shopping and purchasing products—now is the time to capitalize on this trend. You have an amazing opportunity to make great sales by following the advice presented to you in this book.

There are a lot of businesses today that are using Instagram to promote their brands and make sales, but not all are successful. This platform contains some obscure aspects that need to be acknowledged if you want your campaigns to reach their full potential.

You'll also learn how this social media platform works, how your business can benefit from it, how to use its features (new and old) to create mind-boggling content, how to reach potential customers, and convince users to buy your products or services, and keep them engaged. You'll also find a few secret tactics to help you to stay ahead of every other brand in your discipline, as well as some predictions that are highly likely to turn into trends this year.

If you want to understand these factors and their benefits in detail and make your brand name a huge success, then you've picked up the right book. With the accurate information and reliable resources, you'll be ready to win the Instagram marketing game this year.

SECTION 1: INSTAGRAM ESSENTIALS

Chapter 1: The Basics of Instagram

Before discussing Instagram for marketing, you first need to know what Instagram is. When this social medium was first introduced in October 2010 by Kevin Systrom and Mike Krieger, no one knew its potential to be one of the top online platforms by the year 2020. Jumping from 100 million users to around 1 billion users, Instagram has gained massive popularity over the last five to six years. Two years after its initial release, Instagram was bought by Facebook for a whopping $1 billion.

As you probably know already, Instagram is basically a social networking app that lets you upload images, videos, GIFs, and stories, at no cost. Users of this app are now amusingly called "Instagrammers." It was initially used to share images of day-to-day life—like breakfast and other meals, vacations, and important moments. Witnessing the massive impact that it had on global users, it was slowly molded into a platform that recognized talent and promoted businesses creatively.

If you're thinking of tapping into this platform and using it for business purposes, you first need to know its basics. Even if you are familiar with it, we'd recommend taking a look at some features that you might have missed.

Creating an Account

The best way to access Instagram is through its mobile application. Once you download it, click on "Sign Up" to create an account by registering with your email ID and a strong password, or by signing up with your Facebook account.

Setting up Your Profile

Next, you'll need to carry out a few steps to set up and complete your profile.

First, you need to think of your username. This is important because you'll be known and recognized by your username or "handle," across the platform. Think outside the box to gain recognition. Whether it's for business or personal use, consider your purpose when joining Instagram, and name your account accordingly. Then, you'll add your profile picture. To do this, find a white circle on your profile where you can add it. You can, of course, change it whenever you want to.

The next step is writing your "bio." You are given 150 characters to describe yourself or what you do, which will be displayed on your profile. You can also mention your real name on your profile, against your creative handle, and add a website link. Now that you have set up your profile and are good to go, it's time to follow friends, family, or other significant people on this platform. You have the "Find Friends" option for already-connected friends through Twitter and Facebook. You can also check the "Discovery" tab that'll show you content according to your preferences.

Uploading Images and Videos

Now, one of the main reasons that you're on Instagram is to share your content with the world. Instagram supports images and video content that will stay on your profile. It's basically a portfolio of your personal life or business. To upload content, you can tap the button of a plus [+] icon and click a picture, or record a video, to share it on the go, or upload an image or video from your phone gallery.

Uploading Images

Initially, Instagram only allowed you to upload images in the square format, which created a lot of restrictions for serious users and content generators. Lately, it has rolled out the feature of uploading images in portrait and landscape modes as well, lifting all restrictions and giving you the freedom to generate content according to your requirements. However, it can still get a bit difficult to determine the correct aspect ratio. This can be solved by clicking on the icon that appears on the bottom-left corner that automatically adjusts the aspect ratio for you. We'd recommend shooting and uploading portrait content more often than landscape, as Instagram is designed to be vertically-oriented.

The platform allows you to upload up to ten images per post, which can be viewed by swiping left. You can also choose the order in which you want your photos to be seen. A lot of people use this feature creatively to show their content in detail.

Filters for Images

After clicking a picture or selecting the image you want to upload, you can click on "Next" and pass your image through a range of filters. There are some amazing ready-to-use filters to vamp up your photographs. If you prefer to edit your image manually, you have tons of options, too. You can crop, change the brightness and saturation, give it a boost, or adjust the sharpness, among many other editing options available.

A lot of users who prefer keeping their photographs professional or who are conducting business through this medium use editing tools such as Aviary, VSCO, and Filmborn. We'd also recommend using any of these tools to make your images and profile stand out.

Uploading Videos

Instagram provides noteworthy options while uploading a video. However, you can only upload a video ranging from between 3 and 60 seconds in length. This is when IGTV videos come to your rescue, about which we'll talk later in this chapter. For the video upload, you can either clip a few shots and edit them together, or cut the video's length as per your preference. Finally, you can choose a cover for your video that'll be seen on your profile when someone visits it. This can be chosen from any moment in your video. An additional benefit while uploading videos is that you can turn off the sound if you don't want it to be heard.

Captions and Tags

Once your image or video is ready with its filters or edits, the last step would be to add a caption, and tag any relevant people in your content. Adding a caption to every post supports your content. However, you're only allowed to put up one caption for an album or a post of multiple images. You can also add the location to every post.

Sharing Posts

Once you're done with the last step, tap on the "Share on Facebook" option if you want to. Finally, tap on "Share" to upload your post. Once the post is uploaded, you can also edit your caption or tag more people by tapping on the "Edit" option.

Notifications

Your notifications can be checked in the fourth category along the bottom of the screen, denoted by a heart icon, located beside the central "plus" icon. You can check the number of likes and comments on your post through this notification panel after you've uploaded any content. If your account is private, other users can send you a follow request, which can also be seen on this panel.

Your Feed

Once you start following certain accounts, their posts will appear on your main feed when you open the app. You can like posts by tapping the heart icon below them or by double-tapping on the image. There's a bubble icon that can be used to comment on people's posts.

Mentions

You can mention other people or your followers in comments by typing "@" followed by their usernames. You can do this on your own posts, as well as on other users' posts. Your friends or followers can mention your name, too. You'll get the update through your notification panel. If you "like" the comment or reply to it, the commenter will be notified as well, possibly starting a conversation thread below the post. Other users can also join the thread.

Apart from these, you will also be notified about the posts that you've liked through the hashtags that you follow.

Stories

The (almost) new sensation of Instagram, the feature of "stories," was initially introduced by Snapchat. It was then applied to Instagram, Facebook, WhatsApp, and now YouTube. Surprisingly, this feature was a major success on Instagram. Stories are highly engaging and interactive, and they play the role of light content that disappears after 24 hours. Also, stories are designed to be vertically formatted, making it utterly comfortable for mobile users to access and engage with them.

To upload a "story," go to your Instagram home page and click on the camera icon that is located in the top-left corner. Take a picture or a selfie, or record a video. You can also upload a picture or video from your gallery. You can add text, filters, hashtags, stickers, emojis, music, and GIFs to make your content playful. A lot of filters and font varieties are available to make your stories more creative. You can also tag or mention people on your stories, or even put the current location, hour, and temperature.

Additional Features

Instagram also introduced the poll feature, where you can ask your followers to choose one option out of the given two. This allows you to swipe through a sliding poll to rate your answer on a scale of 1 to 10. Another interesting and interactive addition is the "Ask me a question" feature, where your followers can ask you a question or reply to yours.

One interesting feature within stories that have encouraged all the millennials and the Gen Z crowd to become engaged is "boomerangs." This feature allows you to create a short video clip that goes backwards and forwards on a loop. It is highly interactive and has been in frequent use since its introduction. The use of augmented reality through filters and lenses has also held the attention of this audience.

Posting Stories

To post your stories, add in all the features you want to use and tap on the "Add to Your Story" option. You can view the list of people who watched your story by tapping on it and clicking on the number of views shown. If you want to hide your story from certain followers, you can go to your story settings and click on "Hide from People." A good alternative is to create a closed group where you can select a few friends that you wish to share your stories with, and it is denoted by a green circle.

To view the stories, you can tap on the pink circle that surrounds a user's profile picture. You can react to their stories through direct emojis or by tapping on the "Reply" option.

IGTV Videos

When they were first introduced, Instagram TV (IGTV) videos didn't get the expected response. These allow users to create videos longer than 60 seconds and up to an hour, and present them in a vertical format to fit phone screens. The latest updates also allow you to post IGTV videos in the landscape format. When you watch a video on the main feed that is more than 60 seconds in length, it'll show you the "Continue Watching" option. This will direct you to the IGTV format, and you can watch the entire video in its designated format. One recent update from Instagram has prompted it to delete the IGTV icon that rested in the top-righthand corner of the app before.

Explore Tab

Instagram's algorithm functions according to your surfing and search results. If you've shown interest in certain topics or viewed posts or videos in a particular category, Instagram will categorize those topics for you and show you relevant content. For instance, if you've searched for fitness, home décor, travel, and recipes, your "Explore" tab (which is the second icon on the bottom panel) will show you those categories and relevant posts that you would like. It gives you a chance to discover accounts you may be interested in.

Direct Messages

Direct messages, or DMs, allow you to send posts to your friends and followers. It is denoted by the arrow button at the bottom of every post. You can also start a conversation within the messages panel. If you aren't following people who are following you, their DMs will reach you in the form of "Requests." It's up to you whether you want to allow the conversation or not. DMs are a great way to conduct interaction.

Other Features

Tags and Photos of You

This is when your friends or followers tag you in their posts. When you visit your profile, you'll notice three icons. The first one is to view your photos in thumbnails of 3x3. The second icon "Posts" lets you see all of your posts as photo tiles that you can scroll through. The fourth icon "Tagged" will show the pictures and videos in which you have been tagged by other users. You can remove the tag from the post and hide it if you don't want it to be seen on your profile. You can also view your followers' tagged pictures by visiting their profiles.

You can tag your friends in a post while preparing it for upload. Click on the option for tagging, tap on your post, and type your friend's username. When the post is uploaded, you can check the tag by tapping the image and clicking on it.

Hashtags

When you're writing your caption before posting any image or video, you can add up to 30 hashtags to boost your profile. Hashtags allow your posts to be seen and discovered by other users because popular hashtags are categorized in a different album within the "Explore" bar. It gives the users who are searching for content within your niche the opportunity to explore your profile. A useful Instagram feature is that you can simply type "#," and you'll be provided with popular hashtags within your category. Still, be sure to stay relevant and use specific hashtags to target your audience. You can also follow certain hashtags that will appear in your feed from various accounts that frequently use and post their content with that hashtag.

Multiple Accounts

This amazing feature, which was introduced in February 2016, lets you use multiple accounts. Offering you the advantage of creating and switching up to five accounts simultaneously, this feature is beneficial to those who want to keep their personal and professional portfolios separate. To create a new account, you can go to your profile and tap on settings. You'll find an "Add an Account" option. Click on it to repeat the process to create more accounts. When you visit your profile, you'll get an option to switch between your active accounts through an arrowed list.

Instagram Live

This feature is extremely useful for "influencers" and people who want to create engagement with their followers. Instagram Live lets you record videos of live events and happenings in real-time. Your viewers can also interact with you through comments and likes, letting you know about their opinions or questions.

Instagram Web

The web version of this platform, instagram.com, can also be used as the web version on any device. Since it doesn't allow uploading any content, most users prefer using the app version. It doesn't provide any additional benefits apart from getting embed codes.

Account Privacy

Lastly, if you want your content to be seen and discovered all over the world, go to your account settings through your profile, click on "Privacy" > "Account Privacy," and turn off the "Private Account" option. This will give you a chance to showcase your portfolio to the world and increase your chances of being recognized sooner.

These are the basics that you need to know if you're new to this social media platform and before using Instagram for marketing. There are still a few minute features that you need to learn about, which we'll discuss in the upcoming chapters. In the next chapter, we'll go through the benefits of using Instagram for business and marketing.

Chapter 2: Why Use Instagram for Your Business

When we get bored, the first thing that most of us do is pick up our phones and tap on Instagram. This social media platform has become such a common part of our daily lives that most brands and marketers are making complete use of this fact, building their brand identity through this free and useful tool. Instagram has proven to be one of the top and most successful platforms to drive sales and create maximum brand awareness.

As we discussed previously, Instagram has had a massive leap in the number of followers who use this platform for personal, creative, and professional purposes. Lately, a lot of brands have made Instagram their primary tool to drive their businesses. There's so much to explore and create. It has provided the freedom of advertising and content generation like never before. If your business hasn't been on Instagram until now, it's high time you got into it and started to create ways to mark your online presence. To be recognized in this digitally centered world, Instagram can be your way out.

Apart from this, there are several other reasons why it's absolutely important to tap into this marketing arena this year.

One Billion Users

Boasting a total of one billion active users to date, this social media platform has no foreseeable lack of customers. With a huge number of millennials and Gen Z using this platform for leisure, you can target the majority of the younger audience if your brand demands it, especially since 38% of the total users tend to open and check Instagram multiple times in a day. With so much traffic and viewers that immensely appreciate and accept new ideas and creativity, you can map a lot of customers through this platform.

Target Your Audience Group

Widely used around the globe and by almost all age groups, Instagram is the perfect platform to form and target your audience group. According to an analysis by Statista, the USA has the most users, followed by India and Brazil, Indonesia, and Russia. It is rapidly growing in the United Kingdom and Canada, as well.

An important aspect of Instagram marketing and your target audience is your reach. Even if you have brilliant content and a defined target audience, you won't drive more sales or increase engagement if you cannot reach more people. To reach more users based on their countries, you can tap into the five countries that have the highest reach percentages, which are Brunei, Iceland, Turkey, Sweden, and Kuwait.

As for age and gender, the major age group that is active on Instagram ranges from 18 to 29, which makes up around 67% of all users. This is followed by the age group 30 - 49, which is 47%, and 50 - 64, which is 23%. The age group of 65+ constitutes 8% of active users on Instagram. The gender ratio, on the other hand, is almost even on this platform, with 48% males and 52% females.

All these factors—age, gender, nationality, and the number of active users on a daily basis—make up your target audience. You need to define your group and play your content and marketing strategies accordingly.

Interaction Made Easy

Once you've mapped your target audience, you can plan your content accordingly and develop strategies to grab their attention. The best way of doing this is to create engaging content that inspires them to interact with your brand. A big chunk of followers is tempted to check out brand products and buy them if they feel at ease or develop trust.

Live videos have made interaction super fun for customers and brands, giving them the opportunity to communicate with brand faces and team members in real-time conversations. It makes them feel more attached to your brand and drives more sales. Stories are another way to create engagement; you can request answers through polls, do a question and answer (Q&A) session, or ask specific questions to your target audience. Since around 500 million users post and watch stories on a daily basis, one-third of which are from businesses, there's a higher chance of gaining more followers if your content is promising.

Brands also request customers to tag and mention their friends to win hampers, trips, or certain products. This further helps to gain more interaction and potential customers.

Freedom to Create Various Types of Content

Initially, based on the concept of images, Instagram was actually about portraying your everyday life and showing off your photography skills. Later on, it was slowly converted into a marketing tool. This is because people are more drawn to visual content that is aesthetically pleasing and easy to decipher. Let's see how the three main types of content on Instagram—images, text, and videos—help to get other users' attention.

Images

Images are arguably the best form of visual marketing, and Instagram is the best place to create interaction based on images and photographs. Also, if your business requires putting up more images to showcase your products and support a cause, you're approaching the right medium. This creates your brand's personality and keeps your followers engaged. Creating edited photographs or making collages to present your products or your concept are the most common ways of using images for marketing.

Text

To begin marketing on Instagram, you first need to define whether your brand is visual or not, depending on the concept, products, and brand language you want to create. Even though text might not have the same impact as visual content, you can still incorporate it onto images or write powerful captions to support your style. Also, hashtags count as a type of written content that helps in creating recognition within your niche.

Videos

Video engagement has massively increased in popularity recently. Content creators are looking for creative ways of incorporating their products into short videos that can grab their followers' attention. It can be product reviews, crossovers, interviews, or DIY projects. This type of content is more engaging for almost all followers, and they tend to watch the entire video.

As we have discussed before, the use of stories and IGTV videos is the new sensation among Instagram marketers, content creators, and brands. According to an Ispos survey in 2019, 62% of Instagram and other similar app users aged between 13 – 54 claimed they are more interested in buying a product from any brand after they've noticed it on stories.

The Benefits of Hiring Influencers

The new-age way of presenting your products or your brand face, influencer marketing, is a top-notch tactic that most of the brands use today. Influencers are like mini-celebrities on social media platforms who have a massive following and a great impact on their followers. Brands are realizing the potential of this influence and rapidly hiring influencers to promote their products. Specific benefits of doing so include:

Reaching a Massive Target Group

People appreciate and follow various influencers due to their personal style and consistency. This has helped influencers to develop a specific audience that follows their advice and tips. You need to approach such influencers who are aligned with your product style and have a massive impact on your target audience. For instance, if you're selling skincare products or cosmetics, it can help to hire a makeup artist or a fashion blogger who has a majority of followers that are interested in these topics.

Presenting Your Products in Creative Ways

At times, brands and marketers get saturated and face creative blocks in presenting their products and services. There's so much creativity and so many cutting-edge advertising ideas on social media today that it can get difficult to compete in the market. This is the point where hiring influencers can come to your rescue. These people have built their own language in communicating with their audience, which can be completely different from your content. This can give your products a fresh feel and look, as well.

Proper Budget Planning

Influencers on social media are paid an amount that ranges from $100 to $2,085 for a single image, $114 to $3,138 for videos, and $43 to $721 for stories, depending on their reach and number of followers. Even though it might sound like a lot, these numbers are actually useful in budget planning and cost-cutting. This strategy has been such a huge success, particularly on Instagram, that brands and content marketers in the US have set a specific budget of 69% for influencers who have been successful on this social media platform. So, influencers can prove to be game-changers in driving sales for your company, making them an asset for an effective return of investment.

The Power of Advertising

Instagram holds the massive power of reaching up to 849.3 million users among the one billion active users, with 52.9 million of those falling into the young age group. This creates a major impact on advertising and sales. This social media platform has also introduced extended tools for advertising. Brands can pay a certain amount of money to this platform to showcase their ads or relevant content.

It ultimately aims at getting more views, driving more traffic to the website or mobile application, and creating more brand awareness. Marketers are allocating a part of their budget for advertising content as it has lately been a successful tactic.

Video Ads

While scrolling through your Instagram feed, you must have come across a lot of videos that have the label "Sponsored" on top of them. These video ads are paid for by the brands, and Instagram shows them to users who have a search history related to the respective fields. This increases your chances of selling your products and getting more followers.

Photo Ads

Similar to sponsored video ads, photo ads are single images that show the product or concept. An additional "Learn More" button directs the users to the brand's page.

Carousel Ads

An updated version of photo ads, carousel ads consist of multiple images that can be swiped through to learn more about the product or concept in detail.

Story Ads

You can also create ads on your stories about important dates, events, and new launches, with a "Swipe-up" feature that will lead your followers to your website for further information.

Selling Your Products

With its recently integrated shopping tools, Instagram is a fun and convenient way to shop for most of your favorite products. While 81% of all users depend on Instagram to search for old and new products, 11% of users from the United States exclusively buy from this platform now. It shows even greater potential for expansion this year.

Speaking of Instagram's shopping tools, you can access this feature through a business account. By adding multiple products to an image, you can have your followers tap on it to fetch details about each. It also lets them check out for payment without directing them to a new website or page. This feature has been a hit among the majority of the users due to its convenience. You can also access the "Shop Now" feature that can encourage your customers to at least check out the products.

Users are also tapping into this social media platform to buy new products based on word-of-mouth recommendations or simply upon noticing the quality that is offered. This can give you a massive opportunity to generate revenue and drive more sales than anticipated.

Use of a Business Account

You can take the maximum advantage of using a business account on Instagram while promoting your brand. This feature was introduced in 2016 and has been used by brands and marketing companies ever since to drive insights and compare analytical data. It shows the age group, gender, and nationality of people who have interacted with your posts. This helps in analyzing your content according to the number of likes, comments, shares, and saved posts, and lets you change or tweak it for the next marketing plan to get more interaction. It also shows the analysis of interaction garnered during every day of the week and at particular hours, giving you insight into the right time to post. Basically, all these demographics can entirely change your content strategy and for good.

Even though we will discuss the benefits of using a business profile in detail in the next chapter, a brief highlight would make its importance clearer. It helps you use important information such as contact information and website links, which are very important for any business. You can also promote and advertise your content.

A Creative Way to Portray Your Brand

Before the onset of social media marketing, we never knew that certain brands and companies had a lighter side to them. Sure, there were TV commercials, but those were solely commercial and did not aim at interaction or engagement. Instagram marketing has led users to believe that there are humans behind the top brands. With lighter content like behind-the-scenes videos and team interviews, consumers are able to see the legitimate side of brands and are able to trust them more. Earlier in this chapter, we also talked about how influencers can promote your products or business with a creative edge. You can also use extreme tactics such as holding contests or giving shout-outs.

Instagram offers multiple tools and an aesthetically pleasing theme to unleash your creativity and show any kind of content you want. Your brand will have a target audience that can be lured with content that they wish to see. This social media platform offers you support and a blank canvas to put out your portfolio. The only challenge is to create your own style and brand personality. But once you do it, you're bound to stand out and get recognition. Also, it's completely easy to use this tool, making it suitable for beginners.

Even though this medium has a lot of potential and functionality when it comes to promoting your business, it is getting extremely saturated and competitive. However, it doesn't seem likely to lose its potential any time soon. Since it is designed to be mobile-friendly, this aspect allows users to access the brand's content and products on the go, increasing the chances of interaction and sales. We highly recommend that you build and promote your brand on Instagram this year to gain maximum benefit from the new features and sales tools.

Chapter 3: Instagram Challenges and Changes

While using Instagram is a fun and effective way of marketing and promoting your business, there are a few challenges and limitations that marketers have been facing over the years. It might seem dainty and glittery on the outside, but this social media platform has its own flaws, too. Even though these cannot be deemed as disadvantages, being aware of the limitations can help you plan your content and marketing strategy accordingly.

And while these challenges remain, Instagram has been working on a number of new features, some of which are already being tested in a few regions. They could either work to your advantage or completely change your marketing game.

As you're planning to jump on the Instagram bandwagon this year, we'd recommend tracking the challenges and changes that you could possibly face on this social media platform.

Challenges Related to Instagram

People who use Instagram to display their professional work and business owners who promote their content to potential customers have been facing certain limitations since the onset of this medium. We're pointing out some of the major challenges related to it for you to be prepared and plan your strategies accordingly.

Web Version Isn't Optimized

Originally designed to be more functional as a mobile application, Instagram hasn't been able to deliver a well-designed and optimized web version until now. Even though we can now view new features like stories on the web version, a few features still aren't available, such as posting images and videos. Also, the images and content, in general, aren't optimized to be viewed properly on all devices. Instagram has fewer features on the website than the mobile application, making the web version less convenient to use.

So, in order to post constantly and to update your brand's Instagram account, you'd need to keep a smartphone or a tablet handy, instead of a desktop computer or a laptop. In this case, it can get difficult to maintain working conditions in an environment that's not mobile-friendly, especially if you don't have a dedicated social media team or department yet.

No Clickable Links in Posts

Writing an effective caption can be difficult, especially when most people prefer to access visual content instead of reading text. A greater challenge with Instagram captions is that they don't support clickable links. You simply cannot expect your followers to copy and paste the link by leaving the Instagram interface, as it is inconvenient.

No one, including you, would want to leave the app and browse another website by copying and pasting the URL unless it is extremely intriguing. We need to spoon-feed every tiny detail to potential customers to expect more sales and interaction. You need to come up with more conventional ideas, such as adding the relevant link to your bio or using shopping tools that can direct your customers to your website or the installation link of your mobile application.

This can be a challenge if your content requires your audience to arrive at a specific landing page with every post, especially if you rely on Instagram for generating revenue and driving sales. It can be a bigger limitation when your target audience is above the age group of 35 or 40, as these users generally aren't technologically advanced compared to the millennials or the Gen Z users.

Certain Downsides of Advertisements

Scrolling through Instagram comes with the downside of watching advertisements and sponsored posts every now and then. Since almost every business is promoting its products and services on this social medium, it has nearly reached a point of saturation. After every few stories and around four to five posts, you can see a sponsored post that is based on your recent search history. Certain advertisements popping up on the main feed get too repetitive at some point.

Among all the ads, a lot of them are fake, too. A few startups simply create false ads and promote them to gain more followers and generate more leads by luring users into freebies or heavy discounts. A lot of users have claimed to have fallen into this trap. It's difficult to differentiate between authentic ads and false ones.

Advertising on Instagram can also turn out to be expensive. It can get a bit difficult to set and manage a budget for ads on this platform, especially if you're just starting out. You need constant cash flow or high funding. Unless you're a huge, established business that can easily set a budget aside for advertising on social media platforms, you'll just have to rely on organic traffic and customers who are genuinely interested in purchasing your products through interaction and high engagement. Since the average CPC (cost per click) on Instagram ranges from $0.50 to $1 (the average being $0.61), it can take some time for you to earn back what you've spent on sponsoring your posts, or at least until you break even.

The costs of advertising vary according to the business or type of brand you own. If you own a company that follows a concept based on technology, you might have to pay higher than those in the entertainment business. There's another downside to paying for advertising. When you switch to a business account, you're provided with free analytics and demographics, but there's a catch here. Instagram often reduces the reach and engagement of your posts to earn money from paid advertising and promotion of posts. This can be a big disadvantage to smaller businesses that are already on a limited budget and need more engagement during their initial days.

Limited Target Audience

Compared to Facebook and Twitter, Instagram has less ability to target local markets. It also creates less visibility and doesn't target a major crowd because Instagram's algorithm functions to promote and update content from personal accounts rather than business accounts. A lot of brands cater to all age groups. And with Instagram, it can get difficult to reach the audience that's beyond the age of 35 as this group only comprises a handful of users. Moreover, your posts will target only 13% of this age group. So, Instagram wouldn't be the best platform to promote your business if your products or services target an older age group.

Even though men constitute 48% of the total users compared to women making up 52%, only 32% of the former are active on Instagram on a monthly basis. This can minimize your reach to potential customers if your products are aimed at men. Even if you're successful in reaching your target audience by a minor margin, most of them would simply like, comment, or share. It's extremely difficult to convert engagement into sales—as liking and sharing are rather simple actions when it comes to revenue generation. Even if a user likes your content, it doesn't necessarily mean that he will like your product enough to buy it or have a meaningful connection with your brand.

Since Instagram is officially only available for Android and iOS, users with devices that run on other operating systems cannot access this platform. Also, not all potential customers have access to or use Instagram. Some users have lately been realizing the addiction that is caused by social media, and are either going on a "social media detox" or uninstalling apps. Still, it is safe to say that these are only a handful of accounts that hardly make any difference in the grand scheme of things.

Lack of Privacy Settings

One of the privacy settings that we all want and are hoping to access in the future is privacy concerning each post. At present, we're unable to make certain posts private and others public according to our preferences. You can only set your entire account to private or public. As for hiding content, you can either archive your posts—and add them back to your profile later if you want—or delete them entirely.

Changes Expected to Occur on the Platform in 2020

While we witnessed major changes in 2019, such as the introduction of dark mode, the "Restrict" feature to block hateful comments, and the countdown timer on stories, among several others, we still have a lot more to look forward to this year and can plan ahead accordingly.

Hiding "Likes" from Posts

In 2019, the platform started testing its new feature of hiding likes on posts in a few countries, including Italy, Australia, and now the United States. Instagram announced it was taking this massive step to reduce comparison and cyberbullying, and make the platform more than just a race for likes. Even though it might affect the engagement and interaction of followers with brands in some ways, the features of commenting, sharing, and interacting through stories and live videos will remain, keeping the engagement intact. Even before the feature rolls out globally, a few brands are already worried about the loss of interaction it could cause. However, it is important to note that you will still be able to view the number of likes that you've received on your posts; it'll just be invisible to other users.

This could lead to a change that all brands could benefit from—the restriction of fake accounts and bots that try to hack handles with more followers or engagement, and take over their genuine content. These changes have been successful in most of the countries they were tried in, and could possibly be introduced to all countries that use Instagram this year. So, we'd suggest planning your marketing and content strategies accordingly.

Insights for Hashtags

Using hashtags has been a common strategy to increase visibility on various social media platforms. Instagram allows you to add up to 30 hashtags to your caption below the post. While a few marketing experts advocate for adding only famous hashtags in order to be seen in the "Explore" feed and be categorized easily within your niche, some suggest creating your own hashtags and experimenting with them. Once your unique hashtag gains traction and gets recognized easily, it helps to create brand awareness and mark brand identity.

A recent feature with the hashtags suggests the number of impressions that every hashtag provides you. It helps you understand the use of individual tags and gives you a clear idea of what's working. It is far more useful than the previously collected impressions that would otherwise get difficult to analyze. This feature will assist you in creating a clear plan of captions and hashtags for your future posts and diminish the need for relying on web surfing to chart out popular hashtags. We can expect this feature to be accessible to all users around the world to improve marketing, especially brands and content marketers.

If your Instagram has this feature available, you can view the insights below a new post and take a look at the impressions from hashtags.

Creator Profiles

Along with personal and business accounts, creators such as influencers and bloggers are offered an option called "Creator Profiles." This feature will let such content creators have more control over their "Direct Messages" panel with the ability to sort out their messages, and the choice to follow specific data. To switch to a creator profile, you can open "Settings," tap on "Account," then follow "Switch to Professional Account" > "Creator."

Even though this feature is quite new, we can expect a few tweaks or new updates within the category this year. This is because the community of influencers and bloggers is rapidly growing on social media, and they, too, need a specific type of account to cater to their needs. It'll also help them understand whether the type of content they're producing is attracting enough attention or not.

Story Templates and Interface

The latest updates on this social media platform include adding quizzes, questions and answers, GIFs, and stickers to your stories. You might have also noticed the new story templates that allow you to type answers in those empty boxes, making interaction more fun. This year, we can expect an even better interface that'll allow for more user-friendly templates and interactive features, which will be useful for brands to increase interaction.

You can increase interaction by asking simple questions to your followers, such as "What are the books you're currently reading?" or "Which beauty products do you recommend?" The templates that are developed to provide users with an easy and appealing interface will urge them to answer. We're hoping for more such templates and interfaces in 2020.

Instagram Scheduler

Even though a lot of businesses have been using third-party tools to schedule, update, and upload posts, Instagram has recently launched its native scheduler to help businesses flourish on this platform. However, this feature isn't 100% effective yet, because it has a few limitations. First, you're not allowed to schedule your stories, which form a very important part of marketing and interaction campaigns. Second, you'll have to use Creator Studio instead of using the Instagram app to work with the scheduler. Third, you'll need to link your Facebook page to this scheduler so that it can function.

If you think that you're used to the third-party tool you're currently using, and if it already functions well, you can wait for the new Instagram Scheduler features or updates to make it more efficient. But if you're new to it, you can start by using the Instagram Scheduler and become acquainted with it until the new update rolls in. Whichever tool you use, for now, just make sure that it saves you time and makes your tasks easier.

Despite these challenges and changes, Instagram is still one of the most sought-after media apps to promote your business organically. Whether it's a company that is a household name or a tiny mom-and-pop shop, every business has seen some form of success on Instagram by using excellent marketing strategies and producing consistent content. Even though it's not all sunshine and rainbows, you can definitely overcome these limitations and carve your path to recognition on this social media platform.

Chapter 4: Setting Up Your Business Profile

While we've already discussed the benefits of using an Instagram business account, this chapter will deal with all the "hows" and "whys" of using it in detail. Here, we will discuss the details of setting up a business account, along with the additional features and benefits that you might have missed in the previous chapter.

Setting Up a Business Account

Set Up Your Profile

You must remember our instructions for setting up an Instagram account at the beginning of this book. Switching to a business account follows a similar path. You first need to sign in and prepare a regular account, after which you can switch the profile to a business account. Let's discuss the initial stage again, this time in more detail, to help you prepare for the switch to a business account.

- **Basics**

Let's say you're a new user, and you've followed the instructions given in the first chapter to create an account. As we know, you can either sign up with your phone number or email ID and password or use your Facebook login details to link your Instagram account to it. To start with the basic business account setup, you need to add your professional email ID, contact number, and workplace address if you wish clients to approach you. But filling one contact field is mandatory to complete setting up your profile. We'd suggest using your work email ID as it helps you find professional contacts easily, and vice versa.

● Choosing the Profile Picture

Even though Instagram doesn't allow users to view profile pictures in a full-screen mode, it still plays a significant role in your recognition. In fact, it becomes more of a challenge, since the window is only 110x110 pixels, so you need to make sure that you're creating an impact with the tiny display picture. You need to choose your profile picture or "avatar" depending on your business niche and discipline. It can either be your logo or a creative snapshot of your products, depending on the people you want to pursue and your target audience. If you have a lot of personal relationships, you can also use your headshot to make sure that your followers know you and your business.

Nowadays, businesses are competitive and thrive on presenting their best versions online. This is why you can find a lot of creativity put into profile pictures of business accounts, too. This might just convey the importance of having an apt avatar.

● Writing a Compelling Bio

Writing your Instagram bio is a creative challenge. You're only given a few characters to work with, and you have to describe your brand or convey your message in a line or two. It needs to be strong, compelling, and descriptive enough for people to be attracted to so that they check out and follow your account. You also need to make sure that the style of writing goes well with your profile's aesthetic theme. Try to add as many relevant keywords as possible to be ranked among the top searches. This is just how Search Engine Optimization and Instagram algorithms work. If you cannot think out of the box, keep the description simple yet informative, as it could backfire otherwise. Your followers should simply know what you do and what your goals are, which is compelling enough.

While you're at it, make sure you add your brand hashtag and website link at the end of your bio for your followers to visit your web page and increase traffic. It shows authenticity and gives a professional edge to your brand.

- **Finding Relevant Contacts to Follow**

If you've connected your account to Facebook while signing up, you will automatically have a list of suggestions for followers from your Facebook friend list. You'll find an "Invite Facebook Friends" option that can be used to send an invitation to your entire friend list. You can also find friends from other social networks such as Gmail, Twitter, Yahoo!, or LinkedIn.

Another option is to find friends and followers manually by tapping on the "Skip for Now" option. You can always go back to searching for friends on Facebook if you need to find relevant contacts. You can search for people or mutual contacts that have been interested in your business. Send them a follow request. It is highly likely that you'll get a follow back from them. Give shout-outs or hold giveaways to request more followers. Keep on trying all methods until you've established a concrete following base that'll organically reach new followers time and again.

We would, however, advise against buying followers to show a high following count on your profile. It's an inorganic reach that'll break at some point and fail to generate revenue. It's better to have a slow start instead and keep on going until you succeed, which you will.

Pick an Appropriate Name

In addition to the above, we've also mentioned the importance of thinking of an apt username for your Instagram account. It matters a lot because this name will be recognized on online platforms that'll make your mark. It is, of course, advisable to stick to your brand's name if you're conducting business on this social media platform, as it'll be the handle that people will use when they're searching for your brand. It should definitely be catchy, but also easy for users to remember so they can search your name whenever they want to.

If your preferred name or handle isn't available, you can find creative ways of fitting your handle in the Instagram pool either by adding punctuation, additions like ".com" or "I am" in the beginning, or "official" at the end of the brand name, depending on your business category. This, along with your profile picture, will show the professional side of your business and help you make a great first impression. For instance, if you're a fashion brand or a garment company named "Bend the Trend," your account handle can be @bendthetrend.official; or if you're working in a real estate agency, you can choose a username that displays your name with your profession, such as "@timgoldberg_realtor" to differentiate your professional account from your personal one. Try to find a username that's close to your brand name by experimenting with different combinations.

You'll also have the option of choosing the title of the page or page category, in which you'll have to mention the discipline that your company is in. A few examples of common categories include art, technology, entertainment, media, movies, music, restaurants, food, sports, fashion, event sources, websites, mobile applications, local businesses, and many others.

Switch to a Business Account

Now that you've created an account that is up and running, it's time to make the switch. Go to your profile, tap on the three horizontal lines on the top-right corner, and tap on "Settings." You'll see the option "Switch to Business Profile." Tap on it and turn it on. You now have access to a lot of useful features that personal accounts don't, such as running ads and viewing engagement analytics. We'll delve further into these features later.

Complete Your Profile

Completing and editing your profile is a must to keep your account fresh and receive more followers each day. If you've already uploaded a suitable profile picture, a good bio, and your website link, it's time to try a few more tactics such as changing your language or adding links to brands and promotions to lure more customers.

- Connecting Your Facebook Page

If you already have a Facebook business page, you can now connect it to your Instagram business account to be able to use the business tools. If you don't have a Facebook page yet, you'll need to create one.

Create Your Brand's Aesthetic Theme

An attractive Instagram theme instantly creates a great first impression. If you own a company that sells certain products, you can create aesthetically appealing content surrounding them. One major factor that plays an important role in defining an awesome Instagram feed is the color palette. A lot of successful brands use a lighter or pastel color palette in their images and videos. A few also use grids and collages to make it appealing when users scroll through their feeds. If your feed is engaging, users are bound to open your posts, then like, share, and follow your account.

If you feel that you don't have that creative edge, you can hire freelance graphic designers, photographers, or aspiring art directors that fit your budget. If your products or services don't demand or fit into the "aesthetic" aspect, stick to simplicity, and just stay consistent for your content to be noticed. If it's powerful, you're bound to get more leads. Even though we'll talk about content generation and staying consistent in the upcoming chapter, it's important to make a note of it.

Another underrated point is the use of fonts. If your posts use text that conveys certain messages or product information, it is important to choose appropriate fonts that'll appeal to your audience. It's almost certain that you'll use text on your content at some point. It could be text overlays on images or subtitles on your videos.

Promote Your Posts and Share

Since we'll be talking about the types of content in the next few chapters, for now, we'll directly skip to promoting and sharing your posts after having created and uploaded them. First, make sure you write captivating captions. At times, the strength of captions can lead to more shares than the post itself. Captions have made their way into micro-blogging to share personal stories that followers get attached to. To increase the sharing of your posts, you need to make sure that you increase interaction with your followers by engaging them in stories or simply responding to their comments.

Share your posts on your stories and encourage your followers to share them, too. Further promotion tactics involve paying for sponsored posts and running ads. You can set a budget and spend it on the various types of ads that are provided by Instagram and Facebook. These media will either target the audience depending on their search histories or your existing target audience. We will talk more about ads, their types, and how to use them further in this book.

Why Choose a Business Account Over a Personal or Creator Account?

By now, you have a general idea of what Instagram business account analytics do. They provide insights and demographics related to your followers and what they do. Let's talk about them in more detail now.

So, we already know that the analytics fetch details regarding your followers' age group, location, and gender in the "Audience" category. These are also useful in knowing the interaction and engagement that your followers have had with every post. You can do this by checking the number of likes and comments, as well as the shared and saved posts in the "Activity" panel.

Moreover, a business profile offers the look and feel of a professional brand and sets you apart from normal users. And of course, we have the undeniably important "Promote" and "Sell" tabs to boost your business.

The following questions will encourage you to use Instagram analytics and insights when you begin:

➢ What is the total amount of content that we generated over the past week? Is it more or less than what we had generated previously?

➢ Are these posts enough to drive the required engagement?

➢ Who are our followers, and where are they from?

➢ How many profile views, impressions, and website clicks did we generate over the past month?

➢ What is the age group and gender of our target audience?

➢ Which days of the week bring us the highest engagement? What are the peak hours that most users interact with our posts?

➢ How many users are more interested in stories than posts?

Contemplating these questions and their answers can automatically derive a marketing and content strategy plan. You'll be clear on who your audience is and what your followers like, which is often very difficult for beginners to decipher. Create a marketing plan accordingly and keep on making necessary changes according to your data insights and analytics.

Additional Factors

We've clearly understood the important benefits of using a business account rather than a personal or creator account. But there are a few more factors that we haven't discussed yet. If we compare the three account types, here are some features a business account will offer:

➢ Schedule and Auto Publish.

➢ Book appointments.

➢ Promote branded content.

➢ Insights and analytics.

➢ Additional contact options.

➢ 2-Tab inbox.

➢ Check branded content insights on Facebook.

➢ Create and manage ads.

➢ Promote posts.

Booking Feature

A less discussed and used feature offered by Instagram's business account is the booking feature. With the provision of your location and website, all your followers can visit your office or physical location, but they can also book an appointment. Instagram has tied up with a lot of scheduling and appointment-tracking software such as MyTime, Shore, Appointments by Square, Acuity Scheduling, and StyleSeat, among many others. You can also find a "Reserve" feature for restaurants and cafes or ticket selling options for popular concerts and shows.

To recap, here's how you'll use your business profile to promote your brand. Create a profile, revamp it with a suitable display picture and an appealing bio, think of a creative theme and a username, create content, post and promote it, find relevant users to follow, and use tactics to create maximum interaction. The CTA (call to action) buttons like the website link and contact details, along with the analytics and demographics, are additional helpful features.

After so much discussion on setting up a business profile, we're sure that yours is going to stand out from others. Now, it's time to delve further into practical Instagram marketing. We will start with content creation and the importance of staying consistent with it.

SECTION 2: PRACTICAL INSTAGRAM MARKETING

Chapter 5: Creating Consistent Content (That Converts)

The first chapter on practical Instagram marketing will focus on one of the most important aspects of social media: content. Content can either define your brand or completely ruin its image. A sure-fire way of winning Instagram is posting quality content and with consistency. And by consistency, we mean posting at least once a day. Instagram's algorithm works in a way that supports and pushes forward content that is posted consistently, hence giving you easy recognition, more followers, and in turn, more sales. Being consistent is one thing, but producing quality content is another. Both should go hand-in-hand.

Here are some intriguing ways through which you can create quality content and keep it consistent with reaching your goals:

Optimizing for Your Small Business Profile

Since we've already talked about setting up a business profile and optimizing it for a small business, we won't go into much detail on it again. We've just mentioned it here due to its important role in boosting content and turning it into leads and sales. To recap briefly, your username, profile picture, and bio must be utterly compelling, with effective call to action buttons such as a working link to your website and contact details like a phone number or physical location. An important factor that'll lure your followers into staying on your profile and visiting it often is your content.

Taking Quality Pictures

High-quality images are extremely important on social media, and to achieve those, we'd suggest you go through these helpful tips:

Arrange an Appropriate Setup

Professional equipment like a good camera, video recorder, and a laptop are the most basic tools required for taking high-quality pictures. Even though phone cameras are pretty good nowadays, investing in a professional camera will give your photographs the professional edge they deserve. If you don't have the necessary photography skills, we'd recommend learning them to use them for a long time until you can afford a professional freelancer—but more about that later in this chapter.

To take amazing pictures, you'll need an appropriate setup. You need to learn a few basic rules about the setup, such as incorporating natural light, exposure of the image, or capturing a picture at the golden hour. The composition is also important. The textures, shapes, and colors of the subject form the "rule of thirds" that balance the image within the invisible grid for proper composition. Consider your viewpoint and frame of the subject to capture images in the best possible way.

Use Third-Party Apps and Tools

You can use a lot of third-party apps to either edit your images or use readily available photos to manipulate them according to your preferences. A lot of editing apps and software such as VSCO, Aviary, Layout, Adobe Lightroom, Snapseed, Afterlight, and many more are available out there to add soul to your photos. Additional tools such as Adobe Stock, iStock, or Piktochart help in providing professionally shot photographs or tools to create infographics and presentations for your company.

A Few Ideas to Shoot Creative Pictures

Here are a few examples of how different natural elements or concepts can be used to your benefit:

- **Minimalism**

Minimal content is serving the millennials and younger generation with a sense of satisfaction and simplicity. Minimalism has been all the rage lately, with people trying to incorporate as few elements as possible in their picture frames. This approach is aesthetically appealing and grabs the attention of users.

- **Colors and Patterns**

A colorful Instagram feed is always appealing. When you're choosing a color palette before finalizing the aesthetic theme of your brand, you need to keep in mind the type of content you're going to present to your target audience. Sticking to that color palette and aesthetic theme, you can choose subjects that offer a different pop of color to create contrast and patterns that portray certain textures to add liveliness to the frame.

- **Backgrounds and Details**

These two aspects are the most captivating shots within images. Whether it's textured wallpaper or a farm full of colorful flowers, any background that stands out can be used as an appealing backdrop to capture your subject. Similarly, shots of details can also provide your feed with a different look. These are fresh, calm, and professional.

Posting Your Pictures

How to Post Pictures

Once your images are ready, you can start posting them using your business profile. Here's a step-by-step guide on how to do this:

➢ Make sure that you have downloaded all the required images in your phone gallery.

After clicking on the plus (+) sign at the bottom-center of the app, you'll be given a window to click on images or record a video.

➢ Since you have the images in your gallery, tap on the "Choose from Gallery" option.

➢ You can then adjust the size of the image, crop it, or select multiple images if required, for what's known as a "carousel" post. If you download an associated app called "Layout" it also lets you form collages.

➤ Edit the image(s) using the provided filters or manual editing tools such as brightness, contrast, vignette, or sharpness.

➤ Click "Next" when you're satisfied with the filter and type a relevant caption along with the required hashtags.

➤ Finally, add the location, tag people, or other accounts in the image, and determine whether you want to share it to Facebook or not.

Creating Consistent Content

To understand this point better, we're going to consider an example or situation where you're starting a fashion styling company or a garments business. This would help you gain thorough insight and get a better understanding of how to create consistent content. These steps are useful in creating content that will last for at least a week or a month, depending on the amount you shoot in a day. There are many more ways to stay consistent, but in our opinion, this seems to work the best. You'll always have something to post, and it will be quality content.

Step 1: Select the Type of Content and Create an Inspiration Board

Your fashion company will require a lot of photoshoots with models and your brand's garments. This would be your basic content type. To create an edge, you can shoot videos of the backstage or behind the scenes. You could also hire influencers who are into micro-blogging and hand over your social media handle to them for a day.

Once you select and plan out the content you want to put up for the week or the following month, you need to create an inspiration board. It basically works like a Pinterest board that gives you plausible ideas for content generation. It'll also make your content strategies clearer.

Step 2: Create a Brief or a Detailed Plan

This is when you schedule the entire plan along with all locations and respective timings for the photoshoot. Once you know your content type and style, it's time to create a plan accordingly. You'll need to coordinate this with the models if you're hiring any. Keeping a plan handy will map out your entire day's schedule, making it easier for you to move and shoot. This will also help to save time and money.

Step 3: Hire a Photographer, a Freelancer, or Learn the Skill Yourself

If you're a business owner who's just starting out, you'll probably be on a budget. But if you can manage the funding, we'd recommend hiring a professional photographer or a freelancer to carry out the shoot for your website and social media content. If not, learn to photograph subjects using online tutorials or a basic course to save money every time you want to conduct a shoot. Good photography is important when it comes to presenting your products to your audience, and it shows the professional and serious side of your business.

Step 4: Put the Plan in Action

Once you've got the photography tools ready to create content, and devised a plan, put it into action. Try to stay ahead of schedule in order not to be overwhelmed with any obstacles. It's an important day for you as you're shooting to gather a major chunk of content, so be prepared accordingly. When you're done with it, get to editing and preparing your final posts and content for your website and social media at the earliest. Schedule them when you're all done, and you're ready with almost a month's worth of content.

Chalene Johnson's Expert Content Engagement Tips

Chalene Johnson is one of the top social media marketers out there and a popular business podcast speaker. A social-media-savvy entrepreneur, she has some of the best tips to engage the audience on social media with your brand.

Tip 1: Interact with Your Audience

The first and foremost step in creating engagement with your audience is to interact with them. If you create posts that ask questions or demand followers to tag their friends, you'll fetch a steady interaction in your comments section. Try replying to their comments to make your followers feel that they are heard. It increases the value of your brand and establishes trust. Stories are a great way to increase interaction; you can put up polls and quizzes, hold questions and answers, or use story templates. If you manage to create a good amount of interaction on comments and threads, you've succeeded. It's even better if you're receiving personal messages through DMs. That's when you know you've truly succeeded.

Tip 2: Keep Your Content Edgy and Different

Instagram is saturated with a common kind of content now. You can see everyone posting Pinterest-ready images or videos of their products. You need to create content that is edgy and different to stand out from other brands. Users are bored of seeing monotonous content and expect something new every now and then. You need to keep your content different from others and create something that your users can relate to. It can be something personal or heartfelt, for example:

- Sharing Experience Through Content

Brands like GoPro sponsor customers through trips; sharing users' thrilling experiences on its Instagram page. This provides its followers with fresh visual content and creates more engagement.

- Behind-the-Scenes Content

As we've already explained before and will discuss further in the upcoming chapters, behind-the-scenes content has been—and still is—a major game-changer in establishing trust between brands and followers.

- Content That Appeals to Emotions

Levi's Philippines recently created an ad that featured a father customizing a jacket for his blind son in Braille. It was not only successful in winning the Outstanding Marketing Award at the biggest national retail awards show but was also appreciated by the global audience. This really helped Levi's to gain more followers and generate more sales. You can follow a similar pattern and generate content that is heartfelt.

Tip 3: Pay Attention to New Features

Whenever Instagram introduces a new feature, it attracts a lot of attention. Many marketing agencies underestimate this aspect and tend to ignore the new features until they're overused. Chalene Johnson suggests working with Instagram and being updated about new features at every step. For instance, when the feature of IGTV was rolled out, not many marketers paid attention to it. IGTV videos slowly gained traction and have now become a major factor in almost all marketing strategies. Instagram has realized this potential and is planning to put a lot of money and thought into this feature to develop it further.

Chalene Johnson ran a test in which she posted an IGTV video without the preview button, and then a similar IGTV video the next week with the preview button. She noticed that the former video got only 3,000 views compared to 60,000 views in the second video. This shows that we need to use what Instagram is presenting us and listen to what the app has to say.

Tip 4: Don't Just Create Content, Promote It

It's absolutely useless to create content and sit back, hoping the world will see it. Even if you create flawless content that's out of this world, what's the point if there aren't many people to consume it? You need to create plans and strategies to promote your content and get it out there. Whether you need to make it aesthetically appealing or informative, your customers should save your posts for whatever reason.

But don't overdo it. Chalene Johnson claims that watching the same content through cross-promotions and seeing it up on stories time and again bores and frustrates the audience. A lot of brands use only stories to promote their content. Even though a lot of users prefer watching stories to other types of content, promoting your posts every day on stories is ineffective. No one likes to see the multiple small dots that make up ten to fifteen stories for a particular brand. If you want your followers to read a specific piece of text, you can record a short video and incorporate the text into it, instead of keeping the text itself on for six seconds, which will be hardly readable, or repeating it within multiple stories.

As we all know, consistency is the key. Use all the available resources and educate yourself on how to create the best quality content consistently. This is the main factor that'll determine the success of your brand on this social media platform. Define your goals, prepare strategies for your content, and stick to the plan.

Chapter 6: How to Use Hashtags to Attract Customers

Before delving into how the hashtags help in attracting customers and clients, let's first talk about how this massive internet phenomenon came into existence.

History of the Hashtag

It all started with a simple tweet by Chris Messina, a designer, speaker, and an avid Twitter user. His tweet dated 23rd August 2007 read, "How do you feel about using # (pound) for groups. As in #barcamp [msg]?"

The idea behind this tweet, as he explains, was to introduce, to some extent, contextualization, content filtering, and exploratory serendipity within Twitter. Little did he know that in a short span of time, the concept of the hashtag would receive wide acceptance across different social media platforms and become a frequently used metadata tag. While he was inspired by a similar use of "#" on other sites, he is widely credited as the inventor of the hashtag as we know it today.

It may have originated on Twitter, but the concept of hashtags and its potential in grouping similar posts is extremely relevant to any social media platform that deals with quick and dynamic content. So, it wasn't exactly a surprise that Instagram, with its vibrant visual content, took the hashtags to a whole new level.

A simple explanation of a "hashtag" is a keyword or phrase that is prefixed by the "#" symbol, whose objective is to group user-generated content of the same type or theme.

While the advantages and convenience of hashtags are proved beyond any doubt now, initially, people hated them mainly because of how they looked on their timelines. But, before they knew it, hashtags were adopted so widely that nearly 24% of measured tweets contain hashtags now.

A Glance at Hashtags on Instagram

Instagram adopted hashtags even better than Twitter. A staggering 66.6% of Instagram posts contain hashtags. That's two-thirds of all the content that's generated on Instagram! With hashtags being used so extensively, they obviously have marketing potential if used smartly and appropriately. We will see how in the upcoming sections.

According to Mention's *Instagram Engagement Report 2018,* which is based on data from 115 million Instagram posts, the five most commonly used hashtags were #love, #instagood, #fashion, #photooftheday, and #style. However, they were not the most useful tags. That credit goes to the ones that actually manage to boast the highest average engagement rate. Those are #ad, #comedy, and #meme. The #ad, as the name suggests, is used to denote sponsored content, which highlights the power of influencer marketing on this platform.

Other statistics suggest that an Instagram post with at least one hashtag enjoys 12.6% more engagement than a post without any hashtags. This clearly indicates that if you are planning on growing your Instagram account's marketing potential, it is imperative to be on top of your hashtag game.

Why Hashtags Are Important on Instagram

Over the past decade, Instagram, as an app, has undergone several changes. However, throughout the process, the hashtags held their ground. The reason is simple—they are too important to do away with!

Using the right kind of hashtags, targeting a specific audience on posts and stories is still one of the best strategies to achieve a consistent flow of fresh audiences to your Instagram account. The smart use of hashtags has immense potential to improve your engagement rate and the number of your followers, which directly translates into more business for your brand.

A public Instagram account with posts carrying a relevant hashtag will be displayed on that particular hashtag's page. Some users follow the hashtag pages to consume relevant content rather than following the Instagram accounts. This audience base does form a significant source of the traffic to your posts. This is a great way to reach the target audience with whom you had no prior engagement. If you can impress the first-timers with quality and relevant content, they are surely going to be your followers.

For all practical purposes, hashtags on Instagram can be described as keywords with which you can maximize the visibility of your posts. You simply can't imagine building an attractive and highly successful Instagram account without taking complete advantage of hashtags' marketing potential.

Things to Remember Before Devising Your Own Hashtags

First of all, if your Instagram profile is private, the hashtags associated with your posts will not be displayed in the respective hashtag pages. If attracting more customers/clients is your primary objective, then a private profile seriously restricts your chances. Of course, once you gain the required level of popularity, you can afford to go private to exercise control over the type of followers that consume your content. But for beginners, a public account offers much better growth potential.

The structure of hashtags allows for the use of numbers, but blank spaces and special characters are not permitted. Also, you can use hashtags only on your own content and cannot use them to tag posts from other users.

While the overuse of hashtags on a single post may not fetch you the required results—using too many hashtags dilutes the specificity of your content—Instagram permits you to use up to 30 hashtags on posts and up to 10 hashtags on stories.

Types of Instagram Hashtags and Their Advantages

There are different types of hashtags in use on Instagram, and understanding them is vital to coming up with an efficient hashtag strategy for your account. The three main categories are community hashtags, branded hashtags, and campaign hashtags.

Community Hashtags

As the name indicates, community hashtags are designed to bring together like-minded people. It is a great way to establish your own community and gain followers with similar tastes and inclinations. Community hashtags also improve the searchability of your posts.

There are several sub-types of community hashtags that indicate your products or services (e.g., #coffeeshop, #pizza, etc.), hashtags that indicate your professional niche (e.g., #eventplanner, #DJ), hashtags for Instagram communities in your niche (e.g., #carspottersofinstagram, #foodiesofinstagram), hashtags for special events or seasons (e.g., #independenceday, #internationalgirlchildday), location-specific hashtags (e.g., #madeinIndia, #detroitmachines, #italiancuisine), daily hashtags (e.g., #throwbackthursday, #mondaymotivation, #wheeliewednesday), hashtags containing phrases related to your activities (e.g., #carlove, #drivefastdrivesafe), hashtags for acronyms (e.g., #motd—meme of the day), and hashtags with emojis (while special characters aren't allowed, you can certainly employ emojis as hashtags.)

Using a variety of community hashtags on your posts can help you reach different yet relevant communities. For example, if you own a custom car garage in Detroit, you can use the hashtag #customcarbuilderindetroit to cover potential customers looking for a mod-job, and you can also use #lifeofcustomcarbuilder to attract enthusiasts who are interested in your daily life as a car modifier.

Branded Hashtags

Branded hashtags are a great way to develop your brand identity and coverage on Instagram. The hashtag can be your company name, product name, or even tagline. It can also be a strong indicator of your brand identity rather than being your brand name itself. For example, Nike's #justdoit works very well as a brand hashtag. The sportswear brand manages to make its followers use its hashtag, which is a great way to spread the reach and lure in a new audience.

Another advantage of using branded hashtags is that you can keep a tab on the hashtag page to gain insight into where and in which context your followers are using your business's tag. This can be helpful in tweaking your hashtag strategy or even floating an effective marketing campaign.

Campaign Hashtags

Campaign hashtags differ from the previous two types in the duration of use. While the community and branded tags are meant to last forever, campaign hashtags are seasonal or even run for just a few days. If your business or page needs a shot in the arm, campaign hashtags are the way to go.

Needless to say, campaign hashtags are usually associated with new product launches, limited period offers, a temporary partnership, etc. All of these activities can reach their maximum potential with the right usage of campaign hashtags.

Finding the Best Hashtags for Your Instagram Account

While it may be tempting and intuitive to use the most commonly used hashtags like #love and #instagood on your posts, you should know that these tags that are used millions of times don't really work well to bring you a new audience. They relegate your interesting post to a needle in a haystack, reducing its potential to reach your target audience.

The more niche your hashtag is, the better the engagement rate on your post. For example, if you own an Instagram account to promote your custom car-building business, instead of using a generic and common hashtag like #carsofinstagram or #vintagecar, you could use more specific hashtags like #americancustom, #customfordmustang, and so on.

At the end of the day, finding the best hashtags for your account makes all the difference in determining whether you reach the target audience and grow your following or not. There are a few proven ways to find the tags that best suit your business and page.

Know Your Audience's Pulse

Coming up with hashtags spontaneously is not going to help you reach the right target audience. It is imperative for you to select your target audience and analyze their behavior, the type of hashtags they use, and pick the ones that are suitable for your page, products, and services. By doing so, you will discover hashtags that are not only relevant but also double up as keywords that people on Instagram are actually searching for.

Check Out What Your Competitors Are Doing

Competitive intelligence is important in any type of business, and setting up a successful Instagram account is no different. Knowing what type of hashtags your competitors prefer will give you reliable insight into the tags that tend to generate engagement. While you may not need to compete with your rival's hashtags, exploring them will give you an idea of what makes your target audience tick. More often than not, you will end up finding a unique hashtag that goes well with your page.

See What Industry Leaders Are Doing

The top Instagram influencers in your field or the ones who have similar target audiences are on the top because they must be doing things right. So, it is always a good idea to monitor them closely to uncover some high-quality hashtags for your own use. You can learn a lot more from the top influencers in your niche than just discovering new hashtags. Their content could inspire you or even give you new and interesting ideas.

Explore Closely Related Tags

If you're enjoying success with a hashtag, it always pays to monitor posts from others with the same hashtag and search for other tags that are associated with it. Often, this exercise will lead you to other highly successful hashtags that are closely related to your crowd-puller. If you find such related tags, use them to amplify your reach.

Ways to Optimize Your Instagram Hashtags

Like any other search-based channel, Instagram's hashtag strategy should evolve with the platform's ever-changing algorithms and best practices. An excellent hashtag strategy reaches not only a maximum number of people but also the right kind of people for your business. That's where optimizing your hashtags comes into play.

The best way to optimize and fine-tune your hashtag strategy is to monitor the analytics closely to measure the performance of your past hashtags. This will help you increase the number of hashtags that work for your page and business. Instagram's analytics tool, Insights, tells you how many people landed on your page via the hashtags you used. Alternatively, you can use one of the many paid third-party analytics apps like Later, which offers even more insights like which hashtags are driving more likes, comments, saves, impressions, and reach. These services also give you objective information regarding the performance of your new hashtags.

The best way to maximize the potential of a hashtag is to try and get into the coveted "Top Posts" category for that hashtag. This naturally directs a lot of traffic your way. For a post to get into the top list, you need to ensure that it gets a high level of engagement in a relatively short period of time. Basically, it needs to be interesting and viral. This tells Instagram's algorithm that your post is of top quality and highly entertaining.

You can also add your clickable branded hashtags on your Instagram bio so that they can convert into website visits. Also, don't miss the opportunity to add hashtags to your stories. You can do this either by using the text box feature (this lets you add up to 10 tags) or by using a hashtag tool to come up with the most relevant hashtag.

One of the most important Instagram updates in 2018 was the feature that allows users to follow hashtags. This is a great opportunity for businesses to maximize engagement with their audiences. If you can get your followers also to follow your unique branded hashtags, then your posts can appear twice on their timeline—once because they follow your page and once again because they follow your hashtag.

Running hashtag-based campaigns and competitions is another popular way to empower your hashtag and optimize its potential.

How Many Hashtags to Use per Post?

Well, there is no straightforward answer to this question. While some experts recommend that you use as many hashtags as possible to maximize your reach, some believe that sticking to five per post produces the best possible results and keeps things within the target audience. The bottom line is, it all depends on your niche, the nature of your posts, and the width of your target audience base. It is advisable to mix it up until you find the right balance for your unique Instagram account.

Hashtags are the superstars of Instagram. By now, you must have realized the immense positive impact a properly calibrated hashtag strategy can have on customers or clients. It helps you build a long-lasting relationship with your followers, as well. So, we recommend that you keep these points in mind while devising your own unique hashtag strategy.

Chapter 7: Stories: 6 Ways to Build Your Brand

We all have to agree to the fact that there's something about stories that drives curiosity and excitement. It's amazing to see how brands and users try to squeeze in every drop of creativity within their content to stand out. Stories are a great tool for such brands. Among the one billion active users on Instagram to date, around half of them—500 million users, that is—watch stories on a daily basis. Since the advent of stories, people have had more content to watch on Instagram. Not only are they using this app more and staying on it for longer, but they are also dedicating 50% of their time viewing stories instead of posts; so much so that influencers and marketers are publishing fewer feed posts and more stories since 2016, which is when stories came into the picture. Feed posts are predicted to decline even further this year.

If you're already intrigued, that's great, because we're going to discuss everything about stories in this chapter. This includes what they are, why they are popular, why you should use them for marketing your business, and how to use them.

Why Use Stories for Business Marketing?

Initially designed as a means of simple interaction or sharing small glimpses of life, stories were the epitome of light content that users enjoyed watching. Slowly but steadily, businesses and brands started to realize the potential of this niche and used it to market their content. Unsurprisingly, these caught on among users, and the marketing strategies of businesses took off. But what is the secret behind these stories, and why have they become so popular?

The concept of stories was initially invented by Snapchat. Then, it was steadily adopted by Facebook and Instagram as one of their main features. Stories are basically light content that disappears within 24 hours. They are raw and fresh, and they appeal to users because of their essence. These are also extremely powerful to convey information and relevant data. Compelling stories are a great way to enhance the understanding and receptivity between two sources.

Stories are basically designed to be vertically-formatted and take up the entire phone screen. It's interesting to watch content that fits in the whole window. Users no longer have to rotate their phones, squint their eyes, or zoom in to watch content. It's fast, easy, and convenient. It's also a boon to companies as they don't need to stress on producing fresh content for their stories every few months. Followers might not entirely recall all content that a particular brand produces. They might, however, remember the impact or impression that the content had on them. Brands can always tweak or twist old content to present it in a fresh way.

Also, stories aren't necessarily direct ads that could otherwise be off-putting for followers. They often don't have any direct intention to sell products or convince customers to buy any brand's services. We're not talking about story ads here. Businesses and marketing agencies are putting a lot of effort into producing story content that stands out. To know what already works and what will work this year, we've curated a list with some tips of how to use them for marketing your business.

But before that, let's talk about how to create a simple story.

How to Create Stories

Creating stories isn't rocket science, obviously. Follow these simple steps, and you'll be good to go.

Step 1: Capturing Content

Open the Instagram app, and you'll notice a camera icon on the top-left corner. Tap on it, and the window will direct you to the camera function to record your content. A big circle placed on the bottom center of the window is used to either shoot an image or record a video by holding it down to film. You can also upload an image or video from your phone gallery by accessing the tiny thumbnail on the bottom-left corner.

Step 2: Adding Features

When you have shot or decided what content to upload, you need to set the viewing frame. This is what your followers will see when they tap on your story. You can either leave it to cover the entire screen or pinch the image and zoom it in or out. Next, you can add various features such as text, location, and temperature by using the third icon on the top. To enhance it, you can add fun features such as stickers, GIFs, or even mentions and tags.

Step 3: Uploading It

After preparing the frame and adding all the required features, press the "Add to Story" button. You can decide whether to hide it from someone or form a closed group to share it with only chosen followers. You can also add the snaps or videos to your highlight panel.

After you're done, you can check the number of followers that viewed your story by clicking on it once it has been uploaded.

---

6 Ways to Use Stories for Your Brand

1. Boomerang and Hyperlapse

Boomerang and Hyperlapse are fun ways to create engagement with your stories. Boomerangs are short videos or GIFs that create a back-and-forth loop of the captured moments. They are majorly used by the younger generation, mostly within stories. Hyperlapse is another creative feature that captures short time-lapse videos. The app uses your smartphone's accelerometer to capture smooth videos and create a hyperlapse. These two tactics are useful in creating digestible content that is truly engaging.

2. Contests or Giveaways

As we've previously mentioned, contests and giveaways are the best way to create major engagement and encourage people to follow your brand. A lot of businesses realize the importance of giving away free items to generate sales and revenue. How this works is that you announce contests to win free trips or your newly launched products by requesting your followers to follow and subscribe to your page, and share it with a number of other friends. This helps you gain more followers and basically a lot of potential customers. Contests and giveaways have gained a lot of traction lately, and we'd highly recommend using this tactic to lure more customers.

3. Converting Your Blog into Stories

A lot of brands run blogs on their websites that contain information about their products or their discipline. Even though they may have excellent content, visibility decreases due to the saturation in the market. To overcome this issue, you can use the feature of stories to drive more traffic to your blog. At times, you just want to make your customers aware of the information that your blog provides, which can be reflected in your stories in bits and pieces. You can plan a bunch of stories on a particular day during the week and assign a blog post to each, using creative infographics and a link to the post. This leads to improved brand awareness and more traffic to your blog or website.

4. Polls or Q&As

Poll stickers and emoji slider stickers are the new way to create engagement with your audience. These are used to ask questions to customers or demand their opinions. Polls include two options that need to be answered by the story viewer. Users can also react to stories by voicing their opinion on any question by sliding the emoji. It shows the reaction percentage by other users. Poll questions like "Which product do you prefer out of the two?" or "Which outfit would you prefer?" can easily compel your audience to answer. You can also use the feature of conducting quizzes or a set of Q&As by presenting a question and giving four options with a correct answer among A, B, C, and D. A great example of a brand that constantly uses polls and emoji sliders is Lush Cosmetics. The brand has figured out its way of creating powerful interaction with their customers, which helps in driving more sales.

5. Adding Links to Stories

After reaching 10,000 followers, Instagram gives you the option of adding links to your stories. This solves a huge problem: the inability to add clickable links to your posts. Whether it's your blog article, newly launched products, or an update to your mobile application, you can add the link to your story after sharing relevant information on it. This grabs the attention of your followers and evokes curiosity in them. An amazing aspect of this feature is that users don't need to leave the Instagram interface; instead, the link directly opens within the app, making it completely convenient for them. It also increases footfall and traffic on your website, helping to significantly increase sales.

6. Story Highlights

Even though stories are disappearing content that lasts only up to 24 hours, you can permanently keep them on your feed by adding them to your highlights. There's an option called "Add to Highlight" at the bottom of the story. You can create a highlight panel with a title that'll act as an album of your favorite or important stories. There's no limitation to the number of highlights panels or the number of stories in each album. It's an amazing way to keep your important brand moments highlighted on your feed. This is specifically useful when you've covered important events during your journey and want to keep them visible throughout.

Ways to Drive More Traffic

Keep Your Stories Short and Sweet

As we discussed above, no one likes a parade of stories that are repetitive and monotonous. In such cases, the majority of users fail to pay attention to your content, even if it is credible. Stick to a maximum of ten stories to tell your tale. Anything above that is bound to have fewer views than anticipated. You need to stick to the point and avoid multiple stories, especially if there's no connection between them. A great tactic to keep your story on the front row is to schedule and post stories after a while, say three to four hours. This lets your viewers find you easily, and you can have more views on your latest stories.

Use IGTV with Stories

While we've talked about IGTV stories multiple times, we're mentioning them again due to the importance they hold—and we will be mentioning them further in the following chapters, too. But here, we're going to talk about integrating IGTV videos with your stories. You can post a link leading to the full-length IGTV video on your story, and add the relevant link to the IGTV description. We already know that you cannot add clickable links on posts, so this feature is extremely helpful.

Create a Story—Have a Beginning and an End

Stories are called this for a reason. They demand that you tell a story that's alluring, captivating, and interesting. You have a blank canvas to produce short, creative anecdotes that can create a lasting impression on your followers. While you're storyboarding your content, try to have an interesting beginning and a satisfying end, with content that resonates with the viewers. Even if you're posting stories during no fixed hours that are spread throughout the day, you need to make sure that all stories connect. Make sure that they have a good flow. End the stories with greetings or a simple "Thank you" to your viewers.

Create Your Own Style

When you put effort into your content, it shows. Many people take stories lightly and aren't willing to put much effort into story content as it disappears within 24 hours. They don't realize that stories are watched more than posts and leave a great impression of your brand. That's why it's important to create your own style that reflects your brand identity. Pick certain fonts, a color palette, or a theme that looks distinguished and marks your brand's recognition. It shouldn't be monotonous, either. Play with your content, but keep a subtle trait of your brand to make it stand out.

Using Instagram stories for marketing in 2020 is a great step toward reaching your goals. However, it should be noted that these tactics and strategies shouldn't be repetitive and frequent. That's why it is important to build a marketing strategy and content plan that'll instruct you on the type of content to be used beforehand.

Chapter 8: Using Video to Drive Traffic

Now that we've explored images and story content let's move on to another engaging content type, which is video. Video content has lately been a powerful marketing tool, and will further grow this year, as well. Around 80% of people online watch videos for entertainment and information over other content types. You can benefit from this by including video content in your marketing planning. Realizing this, 63% of marketing agencies have already incorporated video marketing into their strategies and content plan.

This is why, in this chapter, we will focus on all the "whys" and "hows" regarding video content.

Benefits of Using Video Content for Small Businesses

Helps in Turning Views to Leads

Among all content, video content has the highest rate of conversion. Around 71% of marketers have claimed that video marketing is more successful than other content forms and that it gives the highest leads. The majority of followers who watch a video are compelled to share it on their stories or through direct messages. This leads to more followers and traffic on your website, ultimately leading to higher sales. Among them, around 74% of visitors tend to buy a product, hence generating revenue. You just need to pay more attention to your content matter, and the rest will follow on its own. Simply put, a view is generally converted into a successful lead.

People Pay More Attention

Compared to other content types, users are bound to pay more attention to video content as it holds the ability to evoke feelings and emotions. It's a great way to build relationships with your followers. It also shows the hard work and effort put behind the campaigns. As discussed, video content that has something relevant or informative gets more attention. For instance, 90% of viewers claim that they learn about new products and their functioning through videos rather than text. This also applies to entertaining and descriptive videos.

More Social Shares

According to statistics, around 76% of viewers claim to share an entertaining video with their friends, even if it belongs to a brand. With the business tools of Instagram, you can view the number of shares of every video and determine the content type that works. Anything that's relatable, personalized, humorous, or creative is bound to be shared more. Hence, it's important to stand out and create something different. A great example of this is animated videos. They are simple, entertaining, and informative at the same time. You can create pitches with freelancers and post animated content every once in a while.

Extremely Descriptive

Not only is video content easy to consume and digest; it is also a fun way to learn. Most content creators try to pack in as much information as they can in a short video of around 10 to 15 minutes. Punchy videos that are even shorter than that are also a very effective way to get new viewers to engage. A few minutes is an appropriate time frame to grab your followers' attention. As mentioned before, most of the users prefer learning about a product or subject through a video rather than reading. That's one of the reasons why marketers prefer to make videos. It's also great for all lazy buyers who'd otherwise refrain from online shopping due to long product descriptions. Videos make it easy for them to make quick decisions and hence help you sell more products.

Good Return on Investment

Not only is video content engaging and interactive, but it's also a great source of ROI for time and money. You can imagine the time, effort, and money required to prepare a video. It's also difficult at times. We talked about the equipment and tools required to shoot a video, and these aren't cheap. So, they add to the cost, and you sometimes have to go beyond the budget. However, since a lot of users engage in video content and are directed to your website, it is highly likely that they'll end up buying a product. This drives more sales and helps in reaching your target. It makes it worth all the money, time, and effort invested.

The Necessary Equipment to Shoot a Video

If you already have the skill set to shoot videos, you just need a smartphone with a good camera to do the job. But a few companies prefer to go the extra mile and use professional tools such as a video recorder or a high-quality DSLR camera. Apart from that, you'll just need a few lenses and a fixed yet appealing backdrop to shoot all your videos, except for when you need a change in your content. A tripod stand and portable studio lights are additional tools to enhance your videos and still photos. You might also need a few third-party tools to edit your videos.

Shooting an Instagram Video

Whether it's a 15-second video to post on your feed or a 10-minute, vertically-formatted IGTV video, we've got you covered with some of the best tips on recording your video content. Now, there are two ways of doing this. You can either casually shoot a video of your surroundings by opening the app and clicking on the center button to start recording, or shoot a professional video using proper equipment, then upload it on your profile. Either way, just follow these steps:

Step 1: Consider the Aspect Ratio

Whether it's shooting for your feed or for your IGTV video, the format is vertical. Considering this, the aspect ratio needs to be 9:16, which is also the perpendicular position of normal videos; so you need to adjust your camera accordingly. Even though Instagram allows you to upload landscape-oriented content now, we'd recommend shooting and uploading vertical content as it is more convenient to watch, thus more commonly preferred.

Step 2: Set Your Camera

If you're using a smartphone to shoot, you're already good with the aspect ratio. You'll just need a phone stand. With a DSLR, you need to flip the camera to a 90° position. Set the tool on a tripod stand and adjust your subject's position.

• Pro-Tip

A tripod ball head can assist you in accurately shooting a 9:16 aspect ratio with a DSLR camera. Fix the ball head to a tripod plate, attach it to your tripod, and fix the camera to the ball head. You can adjust, tilt, or pan the camera according to your preference to have a smooth and proportionate shot. You can also use a camera stabilizer, monopod, studio lights, or a slider to have professional results.

You might also need a microphone in case you want to add a conversation or sound in your video. A small mic is often attached to the shirt or blouse of the person who is speaking in the video. This allows for clear audio and adds a professional touch to it.

Step 3: Shoot and Edit

As soon as you have your equipment and setup ready, it's time to shoot. Take multiple shots and video samples of the chosen subject, according to your storyboard. Tap on the camera screen on the point where you want to keep focus.

To edit your video, you can choose from the row of filters available on the app if you've shot on your phone. You can also use some of the amazing third-party apps to edit your videos with special effects, and to delete unnecessary shots.

To choose music for your video, you can use some of the external tools and useful apps such as SoundCloud, AudioJungle, or Soundstripe. Other useful apps to help you cut frames, change the orientation, and edit the video overall are VideoCrop, InShot, and CutStory, among others.

And that's it! You're ready to upload your video.

Types of Video Content to Create Engagement

Humor and Light Content

Humor is our favorite way of creating engagement! We suggest that you incorporate it into your video content to garner a lot of attention. Preparing content that is light, funny, and catchy is imperative. You can find a lot of young people sharing memes and sarcastic posts all over Instagram. Dive into puns and current affairs, or mix trending memes with your content to give your followers a light chuckle. Using parody in any popular subject can also grab a few eyeballs. This shows the clever side of your team, and needless to say, the younger generation highly appreciates wit and comedy.

Interviews with Team Members or Clients

While you're planning your content strategies, you can consider an interview shoot with your team members once a month. You can either interview different team members in every video or hold a collective meet-and-greet that includes quizzes, interviews, and games with your entire team. Your audience would like to know the faces behind your awesome brand, and it'd make them trust you more.

Video testimonials with clients are the most honest form of content that you can present to your viewers. If you trust your products and are sure that you'll fetch positive reviews, you can try them out. Since they are true, your potential customers would get an honest opinion and would trust your brand while buying your products.

Live Videos

Live videos have proven to be one of the most engaging content creation techniques so far. They come with a lot of added benefits, too. These are easy to create, take up less time, and need no thorough planning. Live videos let your audience interact with you in real-time, without any filter. Your followers can react to your live videos and share live comments. You can also hold interactive sessions by answering your followers' questions, or by handing over your account to an influencer who belongs to your discipline. This will also help you gather more followers from their accounts.

Personalization

When you tweak the content and personalize it according to your target audience, you're bound to fetch more views. One great example is how Spotify rolled out personalized music statistics according to each user at the end of 2019. A lot of users appreciated this type of content and shared it across various platforms. It helped Spotify to gain a massive number of users in the following time period. You can point out traits or understand your target audience to map out customized content that they'd like and appreciate. Something that's relatable is surely going to be successful among your followers.

DIY or Product Description

If your brand involves selling a product, you definitely need to tap into video marketing. A great way to showcase your products to your customers is by making videos about them. Say, for example, you're managing a makeup brand. There are some great ways to play with your products to create amazing video content. Here are some of those awesome ways to do it:

➤ Motion design or time-lapse video to show the most sought-after or newly launched products.

➤ Collaborating with various influencers who have a strong follower base and hiring them to produce video content showcasing your products.

➤ A DIY or "how to use" video.

➤ Surprising facts about your products or the benefits of using them.

Strategies for Driving More Traffic through Video Content

Use Search Engine Optimization

Whether you're using IGTV videos or short videos that will be posted on your feed and stories, you need to follow other strategies, such as using hashtags, to promote your content. But if you're sharing a glimpse of the main video on your story, you need to provide the website link through which your followers can find the video. In this case, your video also needs to be ranked higher on the Google search list to be seen. This can only be possible with Search Engine Optimization. You need to apply certain keywords and phrases to your video title and description, which will optimize it for better search results. The search engine is designed to search for results according to specific keywords and the common word searches of users.

Prepare Your Content Plan

You need to define your content and decide on its type, depending on your target audience. Since we've discussed a lot of video content ideas, you can choose from the options and prepare a strategic plan accordingly. Every content type that you prefer needs to have a purpose and drive more leads.

The next thing you need to incorporate into your content plan is consistency. We already talked about the importance of being consistent in earlier chapters, so you must know the reason why we're mentioning it again. It'll keep your feed and profile in the top searches, and you're bound to be discovered more easily.

Driving traffic through videos is all about finding that angle that your followers would appreciate and incorporating it into your content. We know it's a big hassle to shoot and upload video content regularly, and that's why we suggest preparing a content plan that works.

Chapter 9: How to Sell Your Products on Instagram

Instagram, being a social media platform with over a billion users, carries immense potential for e-commerce business. As we clearly know by now, it's not just about the size of subscribers. At least 500 million Instagram users log into the platform on a daily basis, and around 640 million users (around 70% of the total subscriber base) follow at least one business account.

Such a vast ocean of potential customers makes Instagram an excellent playground for social media marketers and entrepreneurs alike. As a proactive social media platform, Instagram has been making consistent efforts to make the platform conducive to business and shopping.

The recently introduced Instagram Shopping feature aims to help brands and businesses to generate sales and leads from the platform.

What Is Instagram Shopping?

Available in select markets across North America, in addition to the LATAM, EMEA, and APAC zones, Instagram Shopping is providing brands with a virtual storefront where people can explore products via brands' organic posts and stories. They can also discover your products via "Search" and "Explore" features.

And how does it work? Well, you can use tags or product stickers on your posts and stories, and when the users click them, they take them directly to your product description page that contains images of the product along with a detailed description and the cost. The page also includes a direct link to your website where the users can purchase the product. So, in a nutshell, Instagram Shopping channels potential customers to your product page, giving you a great opportunity to convert the leads into sales.

Basically, it makes it a lot easier for brands to highlight the products that are incorporated into their posts and stories. This feature makes Instagram Shopping an extremely attractive avenue for e-commerce brands.

Before Instagram Shopping came into existence, the customer journey on a branded business's Instagram page used to go like this: the customers would follow your page, enjoy the content, and become interested in the products it offered. They would go on to like and comment on the posts, enquiring about the product, and its availability. Ultimately, they would have to visit the product website to try and search for the product they saw on Instagram. It wasn't guaranteed that every customer who got interested in the product due to the brand's Instagram content would actually put the required effort into finding the product on the website and purchase it. This is an unfavorable situation for both the brand and its prospective clientele.

With the introduction of Instagram Shopping, life has gotten so much easier for both parties. The feature has made moving between two different channels (the social media platform and the seller's website) a seamless process, as a simple click on the Instagram post promoting the product will land the user directly on the page where they can buy it instantly. All the branded page needs to do is tag its products appropriately so that the customers can follow them up easily. Naturally, the conversion rate of prospects into actual customers is much higher with Instagram Shopping.

Now, it's time to answer the obvious question:

How to Sell on Instagram

Well, there are two types of paths you can explore. You can place your products on your posts or your stories. They require different approaches, as we are going to see in the following section.

Selling Products through Posts

➤ First things first. Instagram Shopping is still in the process of being introduced across the world. As of now, the feature is accessible only in select countries, and checking if your country is one of them is the obvious first step.

➤ Once you have determined that Instagram Shopping is indeed active in your country, the next step is to connect your Instagram account to your brand's Facebook channel. That's mandatory!

➤ Once you ensure the cross-connectivity between your Instagram and Facebook channels, you can go about setting up your Instagram business account for your brand. You can convert your personal account into a business account by following a few easy steps. Access your profile's "Settings" and click on "Account." Then, select "Switch to Professional Account." Finally, select "Business" and furnish details regarding the category your business falls into and contact information. Press "Done" and your Instagram business account is good to go. A business profile will give you access to various business features and Instagram Insights, which can be used to gain insights into the engagement rate of your posts and page.

➤ The next step is to set up an Instagram Sales Channel on your Shopify store so that you can add products to your Insta posts and link them to your Shopify store. Before you do this, you need to set up your Facebook page and list your products on the Facebook product catalog (using Facebook Shop).

➤ The above step can be done by logging into your Shopify admin page and clicking the "+" button under the "Sales Channels" heading. Select "Instagram" under the "Add Sales Channels" dialog and click "Add Channel." Finally, log in to your Facebook account page to authenticate the Instagram account in the sales channel. Once this is done, Instagram will review your account and give you approval. Should you run into a hurdle, you can always raise a ticket with the Instagram help center.

➢ With all the above steps executed, now it's time to take your awesome products to your Instagram followers. You can simply post an image containing your product and tag your products by selecting "Tag Products" button, and click anywhere on your image like you normally do to tag people. Once you click on where you want to place a tag, a search bar will appear, in which you need to type the name of your product exactly as it appears in your store.

Congratulations! You have finally added a post that can enjoy the full benefits of Instagram Shopping. It is to be remembered that there is a limit on the number of products you can tag on an image, so it is useful to have just a limited number of products highlighted per image. If you want to tag more products in a single post, then you can opt for carousel posts (multiple images on a single post).

Selling Products through Instagram Stories

Instagram allows the brand pages to position their products and tag them on the stories so that the users who are interacting with the stories can directly buy products from their favorite brand stores. Given that 300 million Instagram users interact with stories on a daily basis, selling products via stories is too big an opportunity to miss out on.

Moreover, a recent survey by Instagram found that most users interact with a brand page's stories specifically to keep themselves up-to-date with their favorite brand's activities.

Just like selling through Instagram posts, selling through stories is permitted only in select countries where Instagram Shopping is available. You will need an associated Facebook channel, a Shopify account to which you can add an Instagram sales channel, and an Instagram Business Account.

Once all these are set up, you can create stories containing your products, tag them, and lead your customers to the product page on your website. Driving revenue through your Instagram page is a fun way to operate your business while continuing to build an emotional connection with your prospective audience.

Instagram continues to improve its Shopping feature by adding new features to it at regular intervals. The latest additions to Instagram Shopping include a new "Shopping Explore" tab, a "Shop" tab on your business profile, and the functionality of shopping from the videos.

Monitor the Performance of Instagram Shopping

The Instagram Shopping Insights gives you vital analytics that let you measure the success of your product marketing campaign on the social media platform. The analytics include product views (the total number of times the users tapped the product tags and viewed the product page) and "Product" button clicks (the total number of times people clicked on the purchase button on the product page).

Stand out with Creative Content to Enhance Engagement

Like every type of Instagram page, a branded product page needs engagement to be highly successful. Creating outstandingly creative, entertaining content associated with your products is a sure-fire way of bringing in engagement. Also, using hashtags in an efficient way can do wonders when it comes to engagement. This has been discussed in detail earlier in this book.

There is no one way to find success in marketing your products on Instagram. So, you shouldn't be afraid to mix it up and adopt a trial-and-error method to find what works for your business, specific products, and your target audience. Keep experimenting with your product-based content to keep your audience engaged, interested, and wanting to come back for more. Only if you have an adequate amount of traffic to your posts can you set about converting them into your customers.

Keep Abreast of the Evolution of Instagram Shopping

The early adopters of Instagram Shopping have been witnessing huge success. As we mentioned earlier, the social media platform is striving to improve this excellent shopping tool even further to incorporate more features and maximize its potential. So, as the manager of an Instagram Business Account, it is imperative for you to constantly keep tabs on the evolution of the app and the new updates that are coming in.

Explore Upselling and Cross-Selling Tactics

Ask any veteran advertiser, and they will tell you that it is much more expensive to bring a new customer under your brand's umbrella than retaining the existing one. If you also consider the fact that 40% of e-commerce revenue comes from just 8% of its customers, an interesting picture starts to emerge.

So, it is of the utmost importance to devise a strategy to increase your customers' order value and maximize the potential of your business. This is where upselling and cross-selling come into play.

Convincing customers to buy a product from your brand is the hardest part, but once you manage to pull that off, it is much easier to give them a gentle nudge to increase the average order value. It's not very different from a generic consumer entering a supermarket wanting to buy a few specific items but ending up checking out with a shopping cart full of other items. All you need to do is present the other products from your brand—along with the one they are interested in.

- **Cross-Selling**

Now, let's see what cross-selling is. It's a tactic to increase sales by suggesting related or complementary products to the customers. For example, if you manage to convince your customer to buy a pair of shoes, you can create your content in a way that shows how well the shoes go with a pair of socks and pants, and tag those products as well. If the customer is interested in your shoes, the chances are that they will also be interested in buying accessories that go well with them. Cross-selling should be devised in such a way that it'll add value to the customer's initial purchase and improve their overall buying experience.

It is proven that the concept of cross-selling has the potential to improve your revenue by 10 - 30%. This can be easily achieved by making small adjustments to the way you create your Instagram content based on your products.

- **Upselling**

As for upselling, as the name suggests, it is a tactic where you lure the customer into buying a more expensive and fancier product; upgrading the product they were originally interested in; or adding an additional item or items to their order. For example, if you are in the business of selling bikes and the customer entered your product page with interest in an entry-level model, you could alternatively suggest a better one with suspension, disc brakes, a water bottle holder, all-terrain tires, and so on. Usually, if given a choice, a significant number of customers will be happy to buy a superior and better-equipped product. Another example is offering "must have" bike accessories, like a helmet or riding gloves, at the checkout.

Depending on your product portfolio and sales strategy, you can choose to adopt either cross-selling or upselling tactics, or both of them, in order to maximize your revenue.

Now you know the benefits of Instagram Shopping, and how to sell your products on this platform successfully. So, what are you waiting for? It's time to set up your brand page on Instagram and watch your product sales go up. Of course, advertising your business effectively will play a major role in your success, as well. You can find more about that in the next chapter.

Chapter 10: Advertising Your Business through Instagram Ads

If you are advertising your business on digital platforms, but you are still skeptical of Instagram's ability to provide ROI on your advertising budget, this chapter will change your mind. Sure, Instagram may not have as many followers as Facebook, but it is growing at a super-impressive rate, making it a seriously viable platform for advertising your business.

Unlike other digital advertising platforms, text ads are not Instagram's cup of tea. Here, you advertise in the form of images or videos, and this allows you to flex your creative muscles and come up with really impactful and engaging advertising campaigns. Moreover, Instagram allows you to target the right group of people at the right time with apt imagery.

Many advertisers have already started receiving better ROI with Instagram advertising than other channels. With the right strategy and a better understanding of how Instagram works, you, too, can take full advantage of the platform's advertising potential.

How Is Instagram Advertising Different from Other Platforms?

On Instagram, you advertise by paying to post sponsored content to reach the target audience and expand your follower base. The primary objective of this sponsored content is to improve your brand exposure, increase traffic to your business website, generate sales leads, and push the current leads toward conversion.

As we mentioned earlier, the key difference between Instagram ads and those on other social media platforms is that in the former context, text ads are out of the equation. You need images, a set of images, or videos to take your business or products to the target audience.

Let's look at some statistics that firmly underline the importance and effectiveness of advertising on Instagram before delving deeper into the procedure. In March 2017, over 120 million Instagram users visited a website, sought directions, contacted (called, emailed, or direct messaged) to get in touch and know more about a business, based on Instagram ads. According to the social media giant, 60% of Instagrammers say they discovered new products on the platform, and as many as 75% of them take action after being inspired by a post. Any advertiser would admit that these are some seriously impressive numbers.

Instagram Demographics

Before you unload big bucks on Instagram advertising, it would be wise to gain insight into the demographics of Instagram users so as to be sure that your investment is used to reach the right kind of audience for your business.

About 55% of Instagram users belong to the 18 - 29 age brackets, while 28% are 30 - 49 years old. People between the ages of 50 - 64 constitute only 11% of the Instagram population, while only 4% are 65 years or older. So, if your business caters to senior citizens, you would probably be better off taking your advertising investment elsewhere. However, if your brand deals with products or services that are suitable for the younger age groups, then Instagram Advertising would be an excellent way to reach out to your target audience.

As for geographic segmentation, about 32% of Instagram users live in urban areas, 28% live in the suburbs, and 18% live in the countryside. Women outnumber men on this platform, but the gender gap is steadily diminishing.

Instagram, like most other social media platforms, offers advertisers complete control over their target audiences—like gender, age groups, locations, behaviors, and interests. The app takes advantage of Facebook's massive and well-established demographic data to direct your ads to relevant audiences. This makes Instagram advertising a very powerful tool for advertisers who are looking to target specific niches to prospective customers.

Cost of Instagram Ads

Determining the pricing of ads on digital platforms is not always a straightforward task, and Instagram is no different on this front. There are several factors that influence the cost of your ads and various ways of managing your budget accordingly.

Factors Influencing the Cost

The Instagram advertisement model is based on the CPC (cost per click) and CPM (cost per mille) methods, and the prices are determined by Instagram auctions. This data is obviously confidential. Even your target audience and the feedback on your ads have the potential to influence the advertisement costs.

According to AdEspresso's insight, which is based on monitoring $100 million worth of Instagram ad money spent in 2017, the average cost of CPC ads on the platform in the third quarter of the year ranged between $0.70 and $0.80. Please note that this is just a vague benchmark to give you a basic idea of the costs involved in Instagram advertising. These prices do vary based on the auction, location, audience, time of the day, day of the week, and so on.

How Can You Control Your Costs?

Seeing that ads that target a specific niche enjoy high rates of engagement, Instagram ads of this nature could end up costing you more than a similar campaign on Facebook. According to some advertisers, the cost of Instagram ads could be as high as $5 per CPM. The advertisers can decide how their ad budget is spent. You can either set a daily spending limit or set a lifetime budget and continue running the campaign for as long as the budget lasts. Advertisers can also control the ad schedule (specific time range during the day), ad delivery method (link clicks, unique daily reach, impressions), and the bid amount (manual or automatic).

How to Advertise on Instagram

Now that we have clearly established the marketing potential of Instagram advertising beyond any reasonable doubt, let's see how to set up your campaign. The good news is, if you are already familiar with the way advertising works on Facebook, then setting up Instagram ads is not a big deal at all. It is so easy that they can be configured through Facebook Ads Manager itself.

Are you already advertising on Facebook? If not, we'll walk you through the process of setting up Facebook Ads Manager so that you can run your Instagram ad campaign through it. It is to be noted that Instagram doesn't have its own ad manager, so you need to set up Facebook Ads Manager.

After logging into the appropriate Facebook account, navigate to its Ads Manager section, and determine your campaign goal. The interface is so intuitive that the goals are self-explanatory. The Instagram ads work for goals such as these:

• **Brand Awareness**

Simply select this option, then sit back and relax as Instagram works its magic to take your ads to potential users who are likely to be interested in your business. The platform is secretive about the logic and algorithm behind this campaign, but it does produce results as new and relevant users are exposed to your brand.

• **Traffic**

You can choose either to direct traffic to your website or to the app store where people can download your app. So, all you need to do is select one of these options under the "Traffic" menu and paste the relevant link there. There is not much else for you to do except to monitor the extent of traffic increase and gauge the effectiveness of your Instagram ad campaign.

- Reach

If you're looking to maximize the number of users that view your ads, then you need to first select your Instagram account before floating the ad campaign. You can take advantage of Facebook's Split Testing feature, which allows you to test two different ads to see which one leads to better results. If you are running an Instagram story ad, "Reach" is the only goal you can use for now.

- Engagement

Engagement is a great way to generate leads for your business; hence it is one of the most popular goals. However, unlike Facebook—where you can pay for "post engagements" or "event responses"—Instagram only allows you to pay for "post engagements" at present.

- App Installs

Setting up app installs as your goal is just as simple as selecting any other goal. All you need to do is select your app from the app store during setup.

- Conversion

This goal aims at leading your target audience to take action. This means using ads to drive users into purchasing something from your website or your app. In order to use this goal, you need to configure your Facebook Pixel, or an app event, based on your website or the app you're marketing. Once you finish this setup, you can keep track of the conversions.

- Video Views

The video views goal doesn't require any additional configuration or setup. Video content always requires you to invest a significant amount of time, money, effort, and creativity. It is always a good idea to pay to get more views for your content so that it can put you on the radar of a sizeable target audience.

Selecting the Target Audience

Once you have selected a suitable goal for your ad campaign, the next obvious step is to configure the type of audience to target. If you are already a Facebook advertiser, things will be very simple, as you will have different types of audience bases already selected. If you are not familiar with this, don't worry, it's not rocket science. Here is how you do it:

- **Location**

You can choose to target a specific country, state, region, city, zip code, or even exclude or include certain locations.

- **Age**

You can choose any age range from 13 years to over 65 years.

- **Gender**

You can target men, women, or all.

- **Languages**

If the language you are targeting is not common in your target location, it is better to leave this option blank. Even Facebook recommends the same.

- **Demographics**

This section, which falls under "Detailed Targeting," is powerful and offers detailed configuration settings. It has several multilayered subcategories that allow you to reach a specific niche. Just take enough time to explore all possible options to decide on the group of people to target.

- **Interests**

This also falls into the "Detailed Targeting" category. You can explore several subcategories to find users who are inclined to be interested in what you are promoting. For example, you can target users who like automobiles, travel, a specific genre of movies, and so on.

- **Behavior**

As you must have guessed it already, this also falls under the umbrella of "Detailed Targeting" and comes with seemingly limitless subcategories and options. You can select your target audience based on their purchasing behaviors, their jobs, anniversaries, and so on.

- **Connections**

This allows you to target users who are connected to your Instagram page, app, or event.

- **Custom Audience**

This needs a bit of preparatory effort on your part. It allows you to handpick your target audience and upload a list of contacts so that you can specifically reach the leads that are already in the bag. This option is also very helpful in reaching customers to pitch upselling.

- **Lookalike Audience**

If you are happy with the way your custom audience base is responding to your ad campaign, you can configure the Instagram ad to look for a "Lookalike Audience." This feature will find Instagram users possessing traits that are similar to your original custom audience base.

Once you're done configuring your target audience, Facebook Ads Manager will give you an idea of how specific or generic your audience base is. Too specific may limit your exposure, while too generic may dilute your ad campaign. You can reconfigure your target audience to strike a fine balance before you flag off the campaign.

Ad Placement

Other important points to take into consideration include determining the placements. If you leave it at "Automatic," the ad will end up running on both Facebook and Instagram. If you have created your ad content specifically for Instagram, then you should opt for "Edit Placement" and select "Instagram."

Budget and Schedule

If you're familiar with Google Ads, aka AdWords, the procedure is pretty much similar on Instagram. If you're new to the world of digital advertisements, then you have to implement a trial-and-error strategy to determine your ad schedule, daily budget, and lifetime budget.

Creating Instagram Ads

Once you've gone through all the above procedures, the only thing left for you to do is upload the ad content you've created and kick-start the campaign. Instagram ads can be created in the following formats: image feed, image story, video feed, video story, carousel images feed, and canvas story. Each has its technical requirements regarding size, memory, etc., and depending on the type of ad content, your available goal options may vary.

To conclude, Instagram advertising can be extremely productive for your brand or business. Being a multimedia platform, Instagram allows you to come up with great and creative ad content. Infuse your ad content with personality and contextual relevance, then watch the magic happen.

SECTION 3: INFLUENCER MARKETING

Chapter 11: What Are Influencers and Why Do You Need Them?

Recently, the term "influencer marketing" has gone viral. Considered to be one of the primary marketing strategies in today's social media scenarios, influencers are being hired on a massive scale to promote brands and drive sales. To begin with, the impact of influencers and influencer marketing wasn't so obvious. As more people joined social media platforms like Instagram and YouTube, it gave a boost to bloggers and influencers who started developing a strong fan base and following.

Instagram, among all platforms, has the highest engagement rate, with 3.2%, compared to 1.5% on other social media platforms. This engagement is also driven by the content produced by influencers.

How Do You Define Influencers?

Influencers are like mini-celebrities that literally have an "influence" on people. Every influencer has a specific language and niche within which they are instantly recognized. You can find influencers in all kinds of disciplines today, such as travel or fashion bloggers, journalists, photographers, and public speakers.

As more people joined social media over the past five to six years and started following people who give fashion, travel, fitness, makeup, and life advice, the term "influencer" was born. Marketers around the globe realized this impact that influencers had on their followers, which coined the term "influencer marketing." They started including it in their marketing plans instead of using the old-school, self-promotional strategies. The year 2017 alone witnessed 86% of marketers hiring influencers to promote their brand and drive more sales. The following three years saw a whopping 1,500% rise in the research for influencer marketing.

The world of Instagram has more than 500,000 influencers of all scales today.

What Are the Benefits of Hiring Influencers?

Massive Fan Following

Unless you plan on hiring micro-influencers, who have fewer followers than mega-influencers or world-famous celebrities, you have the major benefit of getting a massive number of potential customers. You will fetch a good number of followers, even if just a small percentage of viewers decide to follow your brand. If your products are promising, followers are bound to buy something at some point, turning it into an advantage in the long run. The fans also rely on influencers' suggestions. For instance, a study revealed that 33% of the Gen Z population who followed certain influencers relied on their decision to purchase a product.

People Trust Their Word

Since people follow these influencers because of their expert opinions and professional advice, they tend to trust everything they say. They somehow establish a friendly rapport with their fans that's informal and trustworthy. More than half of the influencers are authentic and stay true to their words, which is applauded by their followers. A lot of them are also considered to be role models for having established their own identity without depending on nepotism. Marketers take advantage of this trust, as well as the relationship between influencers and their followers, and pay influencers to promote their products. They depend on the fact that any information provided by these influencers is going to be received positively by their followers, which can lead to higher sales.

This type of indirect marketing also gives the consumers a chance to indulge in new products without facing the pressure to buy it, making it a nuanced marketing strategy that has a higher chance of success. Even though consumers are aware of the content being a sponsored endorsement, they still find the advice to be dependable and honest.

Highly Engaged Target Audience

Depending on the niche of certain influencers and their style, they can come with a highly engaged audience. Their followers take their advice and follow them for a reason. If your products or services are targeted to a certain group, you need to list the influencers you wish to collaborate with. For instance, if your company focuses on manufacturing skin products, you need to target the makeup and beauty bloggers within your area or country. In this case, your target audience will probably be the female population within an age range of 18 to 35 years old. This tactic will not only help you in reaching a major target audience but also in creating engagement, which can be very beneficial for your brand.

A great example of a brand that has solely relied on influencer marketing recently, without producing any commercials, is Daniel Wellington. The brand, which is a leading name in its discipline of designing watches, had to take this risk to understand better sales patterns and receive feedback from the audience.

Creative Way of Advertising Your Products

With so much content produced all over the platform every day, followers can get easily bored when they see repetitive posts. Even though it may look easy, it's highly challenging to keep your audience entertained with every post. There are many creative minds out there who put a lot of effort into creating excellent content, which can make the platform get saturated at some point. You can often find yourself brainstorming to be able to produce fresh content and failing to come up with new ideas.

That's when hiring influencers can help you. Influencers have their own style of producing content that is favored by their followers. They can promote your products in their own style and manner. This gives a different edge to your marketing, and your followers get to view fresh content, ultimately resulting in more engagement from old and new followers.

A Great Return on Investment

We've talked about the importance of the return on investment (ROI) while marketing on social media platforms. It takes a lot of effort, time, and money to produce content that can engage your audience. Influencers provide small brands and companies with great ROI, even with a fixed budget. Initially, it might seem expensive to pay hefty paychecks and give away freebies during contests held by your hired influencers. But as we discussed the impact of influencers on their followers, we can anticipate and calculate the ROI accordingly.

According to stats and numbers, you can expect to earn an average of $6.50 on every $1 spent, making it almost six times more beneficial. To have a successful return on investment, you just need to make a definite plan, determine your objectives, and set appropriate key performance indicators (KPIs). Also, it's important to define your main goal behind every campaign. Whether you need to boost engagement and increase your likes, shares, and comments, or you need to generate more sales, targeting influencers, and setting relevant strategies will help you tremendously.

Defining Micro- and Nano-Influencers

As the name suggests, micro- and nano-influencers are those who have a small number of followers compared to the bigger celebrities. However, they still have a major engagement with their followers. Basically, these have 100,000 followers or less. With one-third of the channels belonging to micro-influencers with 10,000 to 100,000 followers, and only 1% being mega-influencers with more than 5 million followers, you can compare their relative and significant impact on the audience and benefit from it.

There's a marginal difference between the terms micro- and nano-influencers. The former has a follower count from 10,000 to 100,000, and the latter from 1,000 to 10,000. Micro-influencers have a better say and are driven to create content that hits the target, compared to nano-influencers. However, we're going to talk about both groups in a collective sense, given their high rate of engagement.

There are so many influencers on Instagram that selecting and hiring a particular bunch can get nerve-racking. Within this population, we'd recommend hiring micro-influencers and nano-influencers, rather than the major bloggers or Instagram celebrities, due to a number of reasons.

Here are some aspects of hiring micro-influencers for your marketing campaigns:

➢ Depending on their reach and number of followers, small-scale micro-influencers are either willing to exchange free products or demand a certain amount of money to promote your products. You need to target these influencers smartly depending on their fan base and demands, and most importantly, according to your budget.

➢ One great thing about micro-influencers is that they are usually quite open and genuine about their opinions. They obviously create amazing content; that's the very reason behind their popularity. Compared to mega-influencers, these people are more connected to their audience. That's because they can easily respond to every comment and private message, making people feel heard and important.

➢ According to statistics, they have a higher engagement and audience reach than bloggers who have more than 100,000 followers. In fact, it is twice or more than the other groups. This gives your brand the benefit of reaching a wider audience with an even higher engagement rate (coined as ER). According to a study conducted by HypeAuditor in January 2019 about the engagement rate within that year, it was found that influencers who had more than one million followers had an average engagement rate of 1.97%; those with

100,000 to one million followers had a 2.05% ER; 20,000 to 100,000 had a 2.15% ER; 5,000 to 20,000 had a 2.43% ER; 1,000 to 5,000 had a 5.60% ER. You can compare the impact of micro- and nano-influencers on the major bloggers by using this data.

➢ Micro-influencers tend to put more effort and time into creating quality content. They discover unseen aspects of your product and create content that's more specific to your category. Not only are their ads creative and unique, but you can also get a lot of notable feedback from their followers. Unlike the content posted on major channels where the feedback from customers often gets lost, the minor channels can give you access to every comment, private message, and insight from your potential customers.

➢ They rely on you, too. As we've mentioned before, a lot of micro-influencers agree to promote your brand and products only for a free supply of your products, instead of paychecks. This collaboration is helpful for both parties. They get to create new content, gather engagement, and receive free products. You, on the other hand, will benefit by saving a major amount of funding within your budget. Basically, they are cost-effective.

➢ Lastly, there is more reach and content creation with groups of micro-bloggers compared to major influencers. Instead of hiring just one or two mega-influencers who take up half of your budget plus the free products, you can target groups of micro-bloggers who will demand less money and generate more content. Instagram has 52% of bloggers who have 1,000 to 5,000 followers; 33.4% from 5,000 to 20,000; 8.2% from 20,000 to 100,000; 6% from 100,000 to 1 million, and only 0.3% of bloggers who have more than 1 million followers. This also increases your chances of running a few successful campaigns rather than one ineffective campaign with a single mega-influencer. Also, this results in more personalization and better targeting of the niche audience.

Influencer marketing is so prominent in this day and age that there are more and more rising influencers within various disciplines, trying their best to gain a solid following, going for collaborations that matter. This is also giving influencer marketing a major boost, which doesn't seem to be stopping any time soon.

Now that you're thoroughly introduced to influencers and the benefits of hiring them for marketing campaigns, let's delve into the influencer marketing process and the results you can expect from hiring nano-, micro-, and mega-influencers this year, in the following chapters.

Chapter 12: The Influencer Marketing Process

Now that we have seen who influencers are, how they can make a positive impact on your brand, and how the term "influencer marketing" came into being, let's take a step-by-step look at the marketing process involving them.

What Is Influencer Marketing?

To put it simply, influencer marketing involves associating your brand with suitable social media influencers who then market your brand to their followers. Naturally, for this to work, the influencers you associate with don't need to have a huge following on Instagram, but they should cater to your brand's niche. For example, using a widely followed influencer specializing in the apparel sector to promote your restaurant is not exactly a sound marketing strategy.

With the right kind of influencers, you can significantly enhance awareness of your brand, because their followers look up to them and usually trust their recommendations. It is reported that 92% of people would rather go with word-of-mouth recommendations by somebody they trust than blindly believe what the brands say. This makes influencers an important asset for your marketing campaign on social media, especially on Instagram.

Various small businesses have reported that influencer marketing is one the fastest ways of acquiring customers and that your ROI with this strategy can see more than a sixfold increase if done right. Of the businesses that are already working with influencers, 59% are planning on increasing their budget for influencer marketing.

Influencer marketing on Instagram can be used to raise your brand awareness, increase its popularity among target audiences, and drive conversions (increasing sales or inducing the users to take certain actions, such as visiting your website or subscribing to your service).

How to Find the Right Influencers for Your Campaign

The simplest way to find the right influencer on Instagram, who specializes in your niche, is by tracking them using relevant hashtags. You can also use various platforms like Statista, which constantly updates the top 10 list of best influencers on various social media platforms in domains like beauty, fashion, food, design, and travel.

Once you come up with a shortlist of influencers you want to engage with, it is always wise to perform some due diligence before contacting them and talking about a potential partnership. Sure, their content may look impactful, and their follower base may be huge, but there are a few aspects that need to be analyzed before getting them on board.

The brand fit and the authenticity of the influencer are very important, or else they will not be able to promote your brand in an honest and inspiring manner. It is also important to note how their content, imagery, and stance will align with your brand.

Of course, there is the matter of quantitative analysis of the influencer's profile. This involves various parameters like:

➤ Number of followers (translates into reach).

➤ Follower growth (speaks volumes about the influencer's ability to bring in new followers).

➤ Like – follower ratio (a measure of the influencer's engagement rate).

There is no point in hiring an influencer who has a huge number of followers without taking a few points into consideration:

➤ Followers may not care enough to engage with the influencer's posts.

➢ Daily follower changes (may indicate unsavory tactics like follower buying or follow-for-follow).

➢ Target group analysis (to deduct bots and fake followers).

➢ Outgoing mentions and posts (to check if the influencer is working with any of your rivals).

The concept of influencer marketing is getting so popular that several agencies aggregating the services of social media influencers have started cropping up around the world, such as Social Match, hi! share that, etc. These influencer marketing platforms act as matchmakers between the advertisers and influencers. They also act as mediators between the two parties and ensure that the whole transaction is fair for everyone involved. If you are new to the world of influencer marketing, approaching influencer marketing platforms to get things rolling is actually not a bad idea.

Approaching the Influencers

Once you've created your influencer shortlist, it's time to reach out to them and establish contact. You can start by following the influencers, engaging with their content, and then approaching them directly by asking for a quote. You can also ask them to review your products or offer to sponsor their initiatives related to your brand, in addition to being open to co-creating content with them. A good influencer will initiate their side of the relationship by trying to know more about your brand and what sort of role they can play in promoting it.

The product review or sponsored initiative would serve as an interview process for both parties. As a brand, you can gauge the influencer's ability to generate engagement with your brand, while the influencer will know whether his/her association with the brand is going to be fruitful in the long run or not.

A successful influencer is also one who receives collaboration requests from top brands on a daily basis. So, your proposal should stand out from the rest, and this means that you need to keep your first contact brief, simple, and to the point. Provide them with a brief description of your brand and its values, along with an outline of the planned campaign and its objectives. This is a good way to start. The time frame of your planned collaboration is also an important piece of information to communicate. If you manage to evoke a response from the influencer, it's time to share more info and highlight the strategy of your campaign.

Negotiating

Once you establish a conversation with a suitable influencer, the next step is to negotiate terms of cooperation. During this phase, it is important to talk about your expectations clearly, so that you can evaluate whether the influencer can help you achieve your goals.

Depending on the type of influencers you are engaging with, you may have to vary your incentives. For example, a micro-influencer in your niche may be content with a free product for review, whereas bigger influencers will have to be persuaded with large payments and even invitations to exclusive events.

One thing many influencers say is, "The advertisers have to give us something of value in order for us to work with them." Money is always welcome, but in several cases, depending on the nature of the collaboration, influencers also accept products or services in exchange for their promotional services. The bottom line is, you need to give the influencers something solid for them to accept your campaign proposal. Asking them to post a story with a discount on your product for their followers and promising them a marginal commission if they sell a product is a type of proposal well-established influencers steer clear of.

At the end of the day, influencers are human beings like the rest of us, and they shouldn't be treated as advertising media. So, communicating with a personal touch and taking a real interest in their personality will help the relationship-building process. This also makes price negotiation easier and more transparent.

Bringing Influencers on Board

Now that you're done negotiating the terms and conditions of the cooperation, it is time to get the influencer onboard. During this process, it is imperative to strike a fine balance between allowing the influencer to exercise his/her artistic freedom and ensuring that they respect certain specifications of the campaign to make it successful. Opting to co-create the content for the marketing campaign with your influencers is a nice way to blend their unique appeal with the authenticity of your brand.

The contract should include some aspects like campaign time frame and deadlines, required hashtags and tags, quantity of content and involved channels, required disclosure of paid cooperation (it's a matter of legality depending on your country), appearance and aesthetics of the content, tone adopted in the content, usage rights of the content under cooperation, exclusion of competitors in posting, and so on.

Campaign Execution

When the campaign sets sail, it is important to keep in constant touch with your influencers so as to keep tabs on the progress of your campaign. Being supportive of the influencers during the campaign and being open to their requests will help you build a strong relationship with your advertising partners. This constant monitoring will also give you valuable insights into the usefulness of your team of influencers. Who is difficult to work with? Who is easygoing? Who follows the preset guidelines the best?

Things to Do Post-Execution

Finally, you have finished running an advertisement campaign on Instagram using influencers. Things don't end here, because you have to determine the magnitude of success the whole operation has achieved. By reviewing KPIs and measuring the campaign outcome, you can determine how each influencer performed and how much value they have added to your campaign.

Depending on the nature of the campaign, KPIs may vary, but generic parameters include the follower growth on your Instagram channel (number of followers who came to your brand's account from that of the influencer), quantity of content under the cooperation, engagement (likes, comments, reposts), quality of comments, media value (the buzz the influencer managed to create around your brand), and mentions/tags.

The main objective of reviewing the campaign's effectiveness after the execution is to identify the room for improvement and to evaluate which influencer was successful and which one was not. This insight would greatly improve your success rate when it comes to future Instagram influencer advertising campaigns.

Retaining the Good Influencers

Just because you completed your campaign and have no plans to launch a new one in the immediate future, that doesn't mean you should disconnect from the good influencers who propelled your campaign toward success. Getting suitable influencers who can relate to your brand and its principles and add real value to your advertising campaign is easier said than done. That is exactly why you should try, by all means, to sustain the relationship with the right influencers that extend beyond the realms of a single ad campaign.

With the increasing popularity of Instagram's marketing potential, influencer marketing will continue to grow in importance for small, medium, and big businesses alike. Your business may be a small eatery in a humble city or a giant multi-national car manufacturer; you can always increase your marketing potential on Instagram by collaborating with the appropriate influencers and dishing out interesting and engaging ad campaigns.

Chapter 13: 5 Influencer Marketing Results to Expect

Even though we talked about the benefits of hiring influencers and the details of the process, we're now going to talk results, accompanied by important numbers and figures. Influencer marketing was such a big hit last year among all startups and small companies that around 90% of marketing agencies gave thumbs up to this brilliant marketing strategy. If you're just getting into a business and planning to promote it on Instagram, we'd highly recommend that you take a look at the numbers and apply them to your strategies accordingly.

Some Important Facts

Increasing Marketing Budget

Two-thirds of businesses on Instagram are planning to increase their marketing budget this year. Upon witnessing the rise of influencers and the success of influencer marketing over the past two years, 63% of marketers are willing to increase their budget to hire influencers to promote their products and brands. A staggering 98% of businesses who have already tapped into influencer marketing plan to keep the same budget or increase it in the year 2020.

Popular Influencer Niches

Among the several types of bloggers that are widely spread across various disciplines, certain niches are very popular among users. The influencers with the highest following seem to be in the entertainment business, with 47% of the total users making up their followers. Next in line are beauty bloggers and celebrities with 43% of users following; then fashion bloggers, having 39% of the total follower count.

Preferred Type of Content

While hiring influencers, you can talk to them about the content type they'd be producing, and you're expecting. A lot of influencers prefer producing videos and stories to images and text, as those sell more and are highly interactive. And for a good reason, 64% of users prefer watching videos, 61% prefer images, and only 38% prefer reading text content. Around 44% of followers prefer watching and interacting with live videos. Thus, when your influencer presents the draft about the content type, you can roughly expect the type of engagement you'd receive and tweak the content accordingly.

Discovering Products

Needless to say, the majority of the users who follow major and minor influencers find out about certain products through them. While 41% of consumers discover new brands and products weekly, 24% discover new products every day through influencers. On the other hand, consumers that find little to no new products or brands through influencers make up less than 1% of the followers. Statistics show that 87% of consumers tend to buy a product after being "influenced" by the influencer's recommendation.

Among many other stats and data, we're sure that these numbers would mark a few expectations that you should have after launching an influencer campaign.

What to Expect When Launching an Influencer Marketing Campaign

Once you've hired apt influencers depending on your category, target audience, and budget, you need to wait for at least two to four months before seeing the anticipated results. Patience is key here. While you're drafting your campaign plan, you need to provide a time frame of three months before you actually start to see results. At times, you might also have to wait a bit longer, so be prepared for that.

Here, we'll present some basic approaches to outline and run a campaign, along with its rough timeline. Even though you've gone through a detailed explanation of the influencer marketing approach in the previous chapter, we'll point out the expectations behind each step and the thought processes that go into planning it.

This will give you an idea of a mockup campaign that would be useful once you begin, along with the results you can expect.

Prepare a Rough Draft for Your Campaign

This will include all the objectives and goals you'd want to achieve through your influencer campaign and the expectations you have from the influencers you've hired. We've discussed a few of these in the previous chapters, but let's dig deeper this time. Here are a few objectives that need to be outlined or expected from your campaign, among others.

Result 1: Increasing Brand Identity and Awareness in General

Since certain influencers stick to ethical causes and public awareness principles, their followers respect and trust every word they say. If you hire such influencers who will promote your brand, your company's name is bound to escalate with more and more people recognizing you and your products. As you know by now, they have a greater reach to the people in your niche audience, who are willing to follow the advice of their role models. Almost half of the total followers tend to follow an influencer's advice in buying products, including six out of ten teenagers on social media. Among all users, 86% of women rely on social media to find recommendations on items to buy.

Result 2: Driving Sales and Generating Revenue

One of the ultimate reasons to hire influencers is to drive sales and generate revenue. We're sure that this would be one of your main objectives, too. Spreading brand awareness isn't enough in itself. Since you're investing a lot of time and money in influencer marketing, you definitely want to boost your sales.

Result 3: Creatively Generated Content

At times, the content generated by influencers can be more creative than that of your own company's content creators and marketing agency. If that's the case, this specifically created content gets added to your creative campaign archives to stay recorded, and it can be reused in the future for further campaigns. This will basically result in user-generated content that can be shared across various social media platforms. Another interesting twist that can be included here is getting content from your followers. Basically, influencers can either hold contests or request their followers to create content using your products. This will not only lead to more sales, but you'll also have more content to post across your social media platforms.

Result 4: Increase in Return on Investment

Depending on their influencer marketing strategies, brands earn around $6.50 to $20 (usually the top 13% of brands) per $1 spent. The calculation for the ROI might seem challenging at first, but you'll slowly get the hang of it once you figure out the way. To adequately calculate the ROI, you can track the performance of each influencer by providing them with specific URLs that have respective discount codes and request insights into the driven traffic. Next, you need to define specific key performance indicators (KPIs) per influencer to understand the engagement, traffic, interaction, and conversions that their content has generated. You can also use some external tools that can easily calculate the probable return on investment and determine whether you'll reach your goals or not.

Result 5: Keeping the Brand Real and Transparent

A lot of brands worry about losing authenticity when it comes to influencer marketing. Most of the influencers are honest and clear in voicing their opinions. However, there are a few bloggers out there who either provide false information or are just asset-driven. A lot of users on Instagram believe that, too. This leads to a fear of losing authenticity among brands. By doing some thorough research and being aware of the influencers you're interested in hiring, you can avoid this. Since most of the followers are already relying on the opinions of certain influencers, you don't have to worry about losing the brand's transparency.

Choose and Recruit Influencers Wisely

Choosing the right influencers for this job is a crucial step to gain the expected results. You can consider these three factors to choose an appropriate group of influencers for your campaign:

1. Know Your Niche and Target Audience

Even though this might sound repetitive, you really need to choose influencers that have a specific target audience to cater to their interests. For instance, hiring a makeup blogger to promote baby products doesn't make sense. Your target audience should be mothers and women in the 30 – 45 age group as opposed to a group of younger women. You should target the group that would actually be interested in your products. Research the influencers within your reach and location, shortlist them accordingly, and then narrow down your choices.

2. Evaluate the Engagement Rate

Depending on their reach, engagement rate, and type of content, every influencer has a different rate of reach and engagement. We saw the numbers in the earlier chapters. At times, it's possible that certain influencers might have more followers but less engagement, but a few might have half the followers and more engagement. In this case, you need to compare the numbers and ratios and choose accordingly. Here, you're expecting a higher engagement rate and more followers depending on the ER of your influencer.

3. Consider Your Budget

You're well aware of the budget perspective involved in influencer marketing. But we're just mentioning it here so that you know what to expect from it and avoid making mistakes. First, you're definitely not supposed to overshoot your budget by hiring an influencer that is overcharging for a certain campaign. There are always better options out there; just be aware of them and do your research. You might want to consider hiring micro- or nano-influencers, as you know the benefits of hiring them by now.

Launch the Campaign and Compare the Results

When you have it all prepared, you're ready to launch the campaign and wait for your influencers to create content and promote it according to the chosen time frame (probably around three to five weeks on average). And as mentioned, wait for at least two to four months. After the waiting period is over, look at, and reflect on the results. It is, however, not advised to compare the results of every influencer you've hired to one another, as they tend to function differently.

These influencer marketing strategies and the results they yield are surely intriguing. It would be a great idea to tap into them this year, as the future seems quite bright. Speaking of the future, it's time to learn more about what 2020 holds when it comes to influencer marketing and the possible scenarios it has in store for your brand.

Chapter 14: The Future of Influencer Marketing

We're sure that you're entirely familiar with influencers, the benefits of hiring them, and their marketing process by now. To end this insightful section, let's discuss what this strategy holds for you in the future. Steadily carving its path to becoming a whopping $8-billion industry this year, influencer marketing is here to stay. So much so that skeptics who initially denied the growth of influencer marketing are now agreeing to the massive jump and success of this market. It is, in fact, predicted to jump up to $10 billion by the year 2022, which is a very short gap for such a big margin.

As we've mentioned before, a majority of brands are keeping the same budget or planning on increasing it this year. A notable example is the brand Estee Lauder. It is planning to channel 75% of its marketing and advertising budget into influencer marketing. Brands are starting to realize the importance of this industry.

Here are a few predictions about influencer marketing that you need to keep in mind. A few of them can also boom as major trends that brands might follow. You're here at the right time; just make a note of these before they go big.

Trend 1: Nano-Influencers Will Take the Spotlight

Even though we defined the various categories of influencers in the earlier chapters, let's present it in a more detailed manner for a better understanding. The five main types of influencers are nano-influencers with 1,000 to 10,000 followers, micro-influencers with

10,000 to 50,000 followers, mid-tier influencers with 50,000 to 500,000 followers, macro-influencers with 500,000 to 1 million followers, and mega-influencers with 1 million followers and more. Until now, brands have majorly hired macro- and mega-influencers due to their higher fan following. However, marketing agencies are starting to realize the importance of nano-influencers.

These bring in amazing ROI through high engagement with a very small investment. We have already talked about the benefits of hiring nano- and micro-influencers, and you can see why we're emphasizing it again. Brands have started their search for nano-influencers who can make a bigger difference with a higher interaction rate compared to the bigger investment and a lower interaction rate in proportion. Also, the quality of content is reliable with these small-scale influencers. So, all in all, the predicted trend this year might be hiring a bunch of nano-influencers that don't burn a hole in your pocket, instead of one or two mega-influencers that pose a higher risk of failure.

Trend 2: Mega-Influencers Will Launch Their Own Lines

Already seeing progress, this trend will continue to evolve further this year. Brands are slowly taking steps toward approaching influencers to collaborate and launch products in their names. Even though brands have to allocate a massive budget to this practice, they are prepared to do this due to the predicted success rate. This is a major step up from hiring influencers one by one. Not only is it a major capitalization move, but also a massive risk to completely launch a new line. It can either be a huge success or a complete disaster.

Well, as per the past experiments, this move has witnessed a massive success. The use of influencers to launch either a significant makeup or clothing line has turned followers into potential customers, driving huge leads, and generating revenue. Influencers are also seeking the shelter of major brands to launch their own lines. They act as the main face of the launch and are successful in influencing the younger demographics. Whichever way it goes, this intriguing collaboration can be predicted to be one of the *greatest* shifts that will be majorly carried out by marketing agencies this year.

Trend 3: There Will Be Events Specifically Held for Influencers

There have already been a few influencer events over the past two years where important influencers of various scales are gathered and awarded with specifically categorized nominations. These work the same way as the big events that are held for mega-celebrities. This trend is expected to grow this year. A number of brands are coming together and sponsoring such events to put a spotlight on their influencers. This will also help them in their campaigns and generate more brand awareness. It can be an awards show, a cocktail party, an informal gathering, or even a trip to a foreign country.

These influencers would either require a special invitation or act as the face for the brand. They contribute by shooting photos or videos containing special moments of the event or trip, and posting them regularly on their social media channels. This provides the brand with even more recognition. One great example of this is the brand Revolve, which sends special invitations to top-level influencers for events like Coachella. There were many stories, images, and videos produced, and the brand got a lot of recognition and engagement this way. This trend seems to be continuing this year, and probably will keep on evolving further, as well.

Trend 4: Influencer Marketing Will Become a Mandatory Strategy

Traditional advertising methods are already less engaging in today's digitally interactive world. Influencer marketing is proven to be one of the top interaction-building strategies, which can create engagement and turn likes and shares into leads. While marketing agencies are experimenting with different influencers and comparing results, they are increasingly planning on keeping the strategy permanent due to its massive success. It is possible to see a lot of brands continuously promoting their products with the help of influencers. So much so that a few brands are signing long-term contracts with select influencers. The reasons behind this are simple. These people are easy to approach and work with and can create more interaction and engagement than high-end celebrities.

This is also because of the relationship that influencers have with their followers. As we discussed, their followers tend to take their advice and recommendations seriously, and the majority of their audience relies on them when buying certain products. It has also gotten a lot easier for marketers to calculate the return on investment. They are able to establish better contracts and have a better understanding of the process.

Trend 5: There Will Be Stricter Regulations and Enforcement

There are speculations of stricter rules being imposed on influencers that plan on collaborating with any brand. The FTC (Federal Trade Commission) announced that they need to be informed about any plausible collaboration between brands and influencers. It was initially taken very lightly by bloggers all across the platform, but they are now slowly becoming more aware and careful about it. Also known as FTC's Influencer Guidelines, these regulations are put forward to avoid unmarked sponsorships and false agreements between two parties. These rules are also framed to avoid fake advertisements that users often encounter on the platform.

The guidelines also mention highlighting the agreement between the influencer and the brand to keep the collaboration transparent and authentic. It can either be done by marking it within your content to make it visible or mentioning it in your videos. However, these also waive off the need to disclose the agreement through hashtags, which was actually not preferred by the influencers. When these rules weren't so prominent earlier, and not many influencers took them seriously, marketing agencies also shunned them. But with the growth of this market, the regulations are expected to get stricter this year.

Trend 6: More Video Content and Podcasts

We've mentioned it over and over again, but we can't highlight the importance of video content enough. It is going to evolve further this year. Podcasts are gaining a lot of popularity because a lot of followers are keen on hearing and being "influenced" by their favorite bloggers.

And as the bandwidth and internet services are improving, more video and audio content is being produced and easily accessed. As we saw that a majority of users (6 out of 10) prefer watching videos instead of watching television, more than 80% of businesses and marketing agencies are now getting into this type of content.

Even though YouTube is highly preferred for video and audio content, the advent of Instagram stories and IGTV videos has increased the caliber and opportunity to create videos on this social media platform. This is a great way of creating interaction and engagement. There were around 29 million podcast episodes and about 700,000 podcasts running actively at the end of 2019. This number is only going to rise steadily this year. And while 51% of the US population has listened to—or prefers to listen to—a podcast episode, you can definitely note it as a great strategy to incorporate into your plan.

There's no stopping influencer marketing this year; it's only going to evolve further in the coming years—unless there is no social media, which, of course, is highly unlikely. Catch up with these trends before they become common, too. It isn't as difficult as it sounds. Just make a detailed plan and follow it in order to know all the potential risks and pitfalls. Even if you fail, there's a valuable lesson for you there.

That said, we're sure that you're now thoroughly prepared to stand out from the crowd and win the Instagram marketing game. Since everyone is creating their niche on this massive social media platform, it is time for you to roll up your sleeves and carve your own path to success. As you've seen time and again in this book, it's not rocket science. You just need to be creative, pay attention to the unseen factors, create a contingency plan, and follow it consistently. Good luck!

Resources

https://www.makeuseof.com/tag/what-is-instagram-how-does-instagram-work/

https://www.lyfemarketing.com/blog/why-use-instagram/

https://elisedarma.com/blog/why-instagram-best-platform

https://blog.hootsuite.com/instagram-statistics/

https://www.techuntold.com/instagram-pros-cons/

https://www.yrcharisma.com/2019/10/22/pros-and-cons-of-instagram-business-profile/

https://suebzimmerman.com/a-beginners-guide-to-getting-started-on-instagram-in-2019/

https://www.youtube.com/watch?v=6_qfwSMo_Js,

https://www.youtube.com/watch?v=K3cY_AGDBgU,

https://www.youtube.com/watch?v=o_q02EtWsUc

https://later.com/blog/ultimate-guide-to-using-instagram-hashtags/,

https://www.youtube.com/watch?v=I3uxif_AIFk,

https://www.youtube.com/watch?v=8JbDFbqguxo,

https://later.com/training/instagram-stories-small-business/,

https://smallbiztrends.com/2019/05/instagram-stories-tips.html

https://www.youtube.com/watch?v=ZfzaLQKXVpg,

https://www.youtube.com/watch?v=d8U01W3DIG0,

https://www.youtube.com/watch?v=B2VxC4v_nxA,

https://www.youtube.com/watch?v=dvEQiuBDSVA,

https://thenextscoop.com/instagram-video-marketing/,

https://www.jennstrends.com/drive-traffic-with-instagram/

https://www.oberlo.com/blog/instagram-shopping,

https://www.youtube.com/watch?v=k0Oe64_eS3Y
https://www.wordstream.com/blog/ws/2017/11/20/instagram-advertising, https://www.youtube.com/watch?v=ePOJhIx8gOo&t=18s, https://www.youtube.com/watch?v=ta8dmGzI50M
https://shanebarker.com/blog/rise-of-influencer-marketing/,
https://later.com/blog/instagram-influencer-marketing/,
https://mention.com/en/blog/influencer-marketing-as-a-small-business-owner/,
https://www.jeffbullas.com/influencer-marketing-for-small-business/
https://www.grouphigh.com/blog/small-business-guide-beginning-influencer-marketing/, https://influencerdb.com/blog/9-steps-influencer-marketing-process/,
https://www.allbusiness.com/work-with-influencers-102360-1.html,
https://blog.perlu.com/how-to-do-influencer-marketing/
https://izea.com/influencer-marketing-statistics/,
https://www.seoblog.com/3-types-roi-expect-influencer-marketing/
https://www.socialmediatoday.com/news/why-the-future-of-influencer-marketing-will-be-organic-influencers/567463/,
https://shanebarker.com/blog/future-of-influencer-marketing/?doing_wp_cron=1577632008.8945600986480712890625

Printed in Great Britain
by Amazon